he plays a harp

a memoir

he plays a harp

a memoir

ROBERTA F. KING

PRINCIPIA
MEDIA

Principia Media, LLC
678 Front Avenue NW
Suite 256
Grand Rapids MI 49504
(www.principiamedia.com)

ISBN 978-1-61485-316-9

Disclaimer
The author has made reasonable efforts to present, document, and provide reliable information in this book. The book remains under review by outside parties including the publisher. However, the author is not responsible for human and mechanical or typographical errors that may be found in the book at this time. Additionally, the author is not responsible for any errors or omissions from the information contained in this book, nor the timeliness of the information. The information contained in this book is not a substitute for the user's independent research and evaluation of the issues and opportunities brought forth.

19 18 17 16 15 14   7 6 5 4 3 2 1

Printed in the United States of America

Cover design and interior layout: Frank Gutbrod
Cover art: Mike Miesch
Drawing: page 84 Mike Miesch
Author photo: Terry Johnston
Photo imaging: Sherry Baribeau

Photo credits:
Roberta F. King: all photos unless otherwise noted
Mike Miesch: page 46
King & Miesch family archive: page 56, 72, 93, 148, 188
Sherry Baribeau/Dirk Wierenga: pages 1, 130, 164, 171, 229, 236, 244
Bill Traynor: page 103
Frederic Reinecke: page 250

To Mike, of course

Contents

CHAPTER 1   Homestretch | **1**

Life Stories

CHAPTER 2   Birth Day | **34**

CHAPTER 3   Reading Aloud | **37**

CHAPTER 4   Blame it on Harry | **46**

CHAPTER 5   Bluffton School | **56**

CHAPTER 6   Swedish Christmas | **66**

CHAPTER 7   Nervous | **72**

CHAPTER 8   Pumpkin Indecision | **78**

CHAPTER 9   Riding Red Man | **84**

CHAPTER 10   Special Needs | **93**

CHAPTER 11   Noah Finds Us a Daughter | **103**

CHAPTER 12   Suspended Belief | **112**

CHAPTER 13   Love Regardless | **122**

CHAPTER 14   Noah Flies Off | **130**

CHAPTER 15   Bay Cliff | **148**

After Death Stories

chapter 16 Homeward Bound | **158**

chapter 17 What I Wrote | **161**

chapter 18 Bravest Person in the Room | **164**

chapter 19 Noah's Funeral | **171**

Grief and Moving Forward Stories

chapter 20 A Thousand Thoughts | **184**

chapter 21 The Gifts | **188**

chapter 22 Leave of Absence | **193**

chapter 23 Permanent Reminder | **198**

chapter 24 Favorite Things | **206**

chapter 25 Let it Be | **214**

chapter 26 A Crush On Him | **220**

chapter 27 Snapshot | **225**

chapter 28 Dirty Clothes | **229**

chapter 29 Virgin Feet | **232**

chapter 30 Christmas Eve Ass Reaming | **236**

chapter 31 He Plays a Harp | **244**

Acknowledgments | **250**

About the Author | **253**

About the Cover Art | **254**

chapter 1 | Homestretch

Through the big windows of the children's hospital emergency room, I spotted Mike leaning on the reception desk. He looked lost. A rush of warm, dry air blew on my face as I walked in. We held onto each other without regard for time or the presence of other people. I felt his chin and beard on the top of my head and I knew he was crying.

"Did you see Noah leave Muskegon in the ambulance?"

"Yes, they put a breathing tube in him. Again," he said. "He looked rough."

"That's not good," I said. "Did anything happen before he stopped breathing? A sign? Did he gasp?"

"No. I don't know. He seemed fine when we left the house. We were talking in the van on the way to the doctor, and then he was just quiet. I looked over and knew something was wrong," he said. "I knew he was dying." Hearing his wavering voice was more painful than I expected. I squeezed his hand and told him I believed Noah would be okay. I hoped this much was true.

Noah had been ill with pneumonia for a few weeks, but he seemed to be doing better lately, and they were headed to his pediatrician for a follow-up appointment. That morning before I left for work was like any other. Noah ate breakfast and I helped him get dressed. I wrote a check for the doctor's office co-pay and I left. How could it be that such an ordinary morning led us here?

An admitting clerk made a call and led us up to Noah's room. We silently held pinkies as we rode the elevator ten floors to the pediatric intensive care unit (PICU).

Noah rested in a big bed wearing just his boxers. There were monitors on his chest and a breathing tube went from his mouth into his lungs. The doctor was listening to his chest and heart, and a nurse was adjusting the settings on an IV pump. I wanted to pull the blanket up on him; he looked cold. He was seventeen years old, but he was still my baby and I wanted to protect him, keep him warm and let him know I was there for him. A visceral mothering instinct overtook me. I reached over the rail and between two monitor leads and placed my hand in the center of his small chest, over his heart. I hoped he could feel my presence.

"What happened? Why did he stop breathing this morning?" I asked.

"How about we go next door to talk and let the team work on Noah," the pediatric pulmonologist, who had been seeing Noah for about ten months, directed us. A chaplain introduced herself and asked if she could join us. I should have known then the news was bad.

"He doesn't have long to live," the doctor began. "His lungs are too full of fluids and he doesn't have the strength to cough. I doubt that even very aggressive treatments will help him in the long-term," she said looking straight at us.

Because of his cerebral palsy and the muscle weakness that comes with the condition, over the last year or so he'd been aspirating tiny bits of food and water. That festering junk caused a lung infection that his seventy-pound body didn't have the power to cough up. Medicine could fix the infection, but Noah needed to cough. She told us that *if*, and that *if* was doubtful, he lived he would never leave our house again.

"He's too fragile," she said.

"No more school?" I asked.

"No, he wouldn't be able to go to school. He'd be on oxygen 24/7 with a facemask," the doctor said.

"But he could eat with us, right? Maybe go out to dinner sometime?" I gazed at a spot on the wall far over her shoulder. I didn't want to look at her.

"No," she said. "No solid food. He'd be on tube feeding only."

"Oh. No. That's not Noah. He loves school. He's a great student and eating…well, he's a good eater," I said, thinking of our family meals: we laughed together, joked as Noah complained when we weren't eating pasta, listened to NPR, and discussed the events of the world and our world. Noah would talk about school, as much as any kid does, and we'd review his papers and notebooks.

"He can't live like that," said Mike, rolling a ring around on his finger. "He'd be so unhappy. We'd be unhappy."

His life, the real living would be over. The news made me feel nauseated. My heart pounded, the room seemed hot and I looked at my feet as I listened. I didn't know what to think or how to pose intelligent questions or form logical responses to her statements. Mike and I pressed our shoulders together weighing a set of undesirable options. I gripped his hand and squeezed off some of my agony. He didn't react to the pressure.

"This is so sudden. I thought he was getting better," Mike said.

She reviewed her notes, took a deep breath and presented us with the clinical details about the condition of Noah's scarred lungs.

We didn't want to believe her, but denying it seemed foolish in the face of what we'd been experiencing over the last year: a helicopter transfer from our local hospital to here (Helen DeVos Children's Hospital) a few months earlier, then back again for a collapsed lung, home breathing treatments three times a day with an electric nebulizer, sleeping with a breathing machine on his face, countless chest x-rays, follow-up visits, long sleepless nights of him coughing and us worrying. Since then, nine months had passed and we'd moved from spring to deep winter. From the day we heard the prognosis until we kissed him for the last time, he lived only eleven days. They were long and exhausting days, but now I know they went too fast.

❖

Over those last days, we timed our PICU arrivals and departures each day to maximize time with Noah and the nursing staff that cared for him. Seeking coffee and news, we walked over from the nearby Renucci Hospitality House before the third shift nursing staff left the hospital around 6:30 a.m., and as the first shift came on. We never left before the second shift nurses departed and the third shift arrived around midnight. We needed to know what we might have missed in the six hours we were fitfully sleeping at Renucci. The promise was if anything critical happened they would call us, but Noah's nights were quiet and the phone didn't ring. After lying in bed talking most of the night, Mike and I would dress and hurry through the quiet hospital corridors, dodging custodians with big floor waxing machines, to ask if anything had changed overnight.

"How were his oxygen stats?"

"Did he sleep well?"

"Did he seem to be in a good mood?"

"Did he ask for us?"

Sometimes a nurse would tell us about Noah's flirting and how he'd persuade her to sit next to his bed and work on charting until he fell asleep.

"Yes, every time I'd get up to leave he'd wake up and ask me when I'd be back," she said. "I could hear him calling me over and over until I returned," she said.

Mike and I jockeyed for the one comfortable chair in the room. When one of us wandered out for coffee, water, a snack, or to ask a nurse or passing physician a question that might give us insight about our son's condition, the other would transfer into the good chair. For almost two weeks, eighteen hours a day we lived in the lull of the PICU. Every few minutes a pump or monitor beeped, an alarm from an empty med bag sounded, a phone rang, or a cart rattled. Staff people talked about their lives outside the hospital and laughed. Around the corner or across the hall, a kid's blood pressure went too high or too low, or an oxygen saturation level dropped and a new machine with a new sound beeped. That din became a white noise of its own, inside and outside of the room. Around the clock, day after day, it went on. While Noah napped, Mike and I would walk to the end of the hall and back, trying not to look into other kid's rooms. When we did look, we'd see parents sitting in their uncomfortable chairs. They looked tired, anxious and sad as they kept watch over their sick babies, post-surgical toddlers and car-wrecked teens. No parents ever expect to find their child a critical care patient and to be making life and death decisions for them. There are no guidebooks or close advisors; we all wing it, trusting physicians, nurses and our own gut instincts.

When Noah was admitted, we didn't know how long we'd be there or what the days would be like. I brought in a laptop, ostensibly so I could work from his room, but once the hospital gave me Internet access we mostly streamed Jimmy Buffett music for Noah to listen to and for me to sing along with. We had a trip to Key West set in three weeks, so we talked about going and how much fun it would be. He loved the Florida Keys and had happy memories of our travels there.

"Remember when we swam with dolphins?" Noah asked me one morning. His voice was softer than usual and had a bit of a wheeze or squeak, like a worn out New Year's Eve horn. It was sweet to hear him speak after a couple of days with the breathing tube.

"Yes, that was wonderful. Do you remember how their fins felt?"

"Yes, I do," he said, as his fingers touched the edge of a blanket. We'd been taking him to the Keys since he was young. It was an easy trip for us, far enough away from Michigan to be warm in the winter and accessible for us and his wheelchair.

We promised him that as soon as he got better we'd head south. It was a lie. He'd never live long enough to make it to Key West. I didn't like lying to him, but talking about Key West brought pleasant memories, now painful in their finality. No more memories would be made. When Noah and I talked about going, I thought about the past, but I could tell Noah was thinking about the future.

After his death, friends asked us if Noah knew that he was going to die. If he knew, we didn't tell him. We didn't even tell him how sick he really was. Out in the hall one morning, while housekeeping tidied his room Mike and I talked about it. In the hospital, life and death conversations take place without planning and rarely in privacy.

"There's no point in telling him," Mike said.

"I think it would be scary for him," I said, glancing into his room. "And there's always the chance—you know, a miracle."

"I'd like a miracle," he said.

"I don't want him to be fearful. Of anything."

I didn't believe telling him he was about to die would have helped him understand or be ready for the mysterious experience that awaited him. Though we never said it, we both knew that the moment of his death would be when we would tell him, and then we told him everything he needed to know.

In the morning, after the physicians rounded and before lunch, I'd read to Noah. Usually, he'd doze off during the middle of a chapter and I'd read on, more softly, while he slept. When I put the book down, he'd wake up. "Mom, don't stop. Read to me." So, I'd continue reading. I tried to read *Huck Finn* but the dialects vexed me, so I ended up reading a few old Lemony Snicket books. Oddly dark and morose, the resourceful kids and dastardly adults made us laugh. We brought DVDs from home and watched endless movies and cartoons. We came to understand the finer points of the sport of curling watching the television as the 2006 winter Olympics in Torino, Italy, were underway. The movie *Grizzly Man* was playing daily on the hospital cable TV network. We seemed to catch parts of it often and when the Grizzly Man was finally eaten, I was secretly pleased. He was wearisome.

Between long stretches of video-watching and hall-meandering, there were blood pressure checks, respiratory treatments and rounds and discussions with the medical residents and specialists. During the first week of his admission, we agreed to experiment with a curious squeezing/vibrating vest device, which was supposed to help loosen the stuff in his lungs and make it easier to cough.

"You look so handsome in black," I said to Noah as the respiratory therapist buckled the bulky vest device around him, plugged it in and the thing began shaking. Within a few minutes, the compressions and vibrations were too much, his oxygen saturation level fell to the low seventies, a dangerous place, and he had to be suctioned. His breathing was labored and difficult; his face paled and his eyes watered. He waved his arms in distress. His mouth was drawn as he gasped for air and he couldn't speak.

"I can't see us doing this to him," Mike said about the vest and the suctioning. Seeing doctors poking a suction wand into our son's airway passages was too much for Mike to bear. The treatment was harsh and Noah cried when we buckled the vest on him again later that day.

"No, don't. Leave it off," Noah said. We tried the vest only twice more before abandoning it. Letting Noah make this decision was the best thing we could offer him.

I found it odd then, but it makes sense now, that a PICU room is designed without a toilet. Critically sick kids don't usually get out of bed. A bedside commode was available, as was a hand-held urinal. While Noah was in the hospital, he needed to use the urinal *a lot*. His cerebral palsy gave him a lack of steadiness in his hands, so we were his urinal holders. Friends would come visit, we'd be having a quiet conversation and Noah would call out, "Mom! Dad! I have to pee." One of us would rush over with the plastic bottle, get him situated and wait. And wait. Standing at Noah's bedside, we'd listen to his assurance that he had to go and we'd stand and wait, sometimes carrying on conversations with visitors—with one hand under the blanket holding it in place. There was nothing wrong with his urinary tract or bladder. He just liked being able to call us, knowing that we'd come fast and that we'd stand by him for as long as needed.

❖

Noah's grandma and Aunt Janice came to sit with him almost every day so Mike and I could leave the room for a bit. We'd dash out for lunch in the hospital cafeteria or out to dinner nearby, but all we could do was talk about Noah. We'd end up crying and hurrying back to the PICU to be with him.

"One of you should go home," said a social worker after we'd been at the hospital for a few days. "You need a break from the hospital."

"I guess so. Why don't you go?" I said to Mike.

"I'd rather stay here," he said. "You know what needs to be done at home." Neither of us wanted to leave Noah. We both knew that with a finite number of days left, we should be together.

I reluctantly gave into a trip home. "Okay, I suppose I could do some laundry. Pick up clean clothes, swap out some DVDs," I said. Maybe the hospital staff thought there were other people in our house, that I could find emotional support from siblings, parents, or another child. The reality was there was no one for me to go home to.

"I miss him already," I thought as I walked up to our dark house. It wasn't the kind of missing I knew I'd be feeling after he died, but more of *I wonder what he's doing now?* type of missing. Wondering if Mike was napping in his room or what nurse might be coming on for the next shift. Wondering what Noah and Mike might be talking about or watching on television. I missed being with them.

The empty house and the inevitability of Noah's death made going home more of a burden than a respite. Other than running the wash and looking through the pile of mail, I was at a loss for something to do. I tried reading and couldn't focus. I thought about calling one of my friends, but that seemed too hard. I didn't feel like talking. I poured a glass of wine, but drinking alone seemed even more tragic, so I poured it in the sink.

In the end, I lay on Noah's twin bed, hugged his stuffed manatee and wondered why he had to die. The glow-in-the-dark stars on the ceiling, the nautical ambiance we created with sky blue and sea green paint on the walls, his old toys, his SpongeBob nightlight and books—all things he loved—now hurt me. I could not fathom that our wonderful child would never sleep in his own bed again. I questioned our medical choices, my care of him and what I was doing in this empty house. I tried to imagine our life without him. I just couldn't see it, or perhaps I didn't want to. After a short night of restless sleep in the quiet house I got up before dawn, made coffee for the drive and sped back to Grand Rapids so I could walk with Mike from Renucci House to the hospital at 6:30.

❖

Sitting quietly in a hospital room for days and nights allows for long stretches of time for prayer and reflection, and I took advantage of it. I prayed silently and sporadically throughout the day, every day, asking God to save Noah's life. I prayed and asked that he be made well again, that we be given a miracle. I asked that he suffer less. I begged God for more days with Noah and for better days without him struggling to breathe and enduring treatments that were supposed to help, but which caused him pain and anxiety. I prayed thankful prayers, for the life we had so far and the joy that Noah had brought us. I asked Noah if he wanted to pray with me. "No, you do it," he'd say, closing his eyes as I folded my hands over his. I'd mumble a vague, hopeful and short prayer as a burning, hard lump in my throat grew and choked me. With a fast amen, I'd turn and look out the window to the winter sky.

"What can I do to help?" asked Joanna, a hospital chaplain. She had been with us since we first came to the hospital.

"Pray for Noah. Pray for us. Help us know we're making good decisions for him," I replied. My prayers were weak, distracted and often went unfinished as I moved on to adjust a blanket or touch him. She took Noah's hand and prayed for him and us. While comfort did not come at that moment, her presence and focused prayers each day during the rest of Noah's days brought us some peace.

❖

Toward the end of our first week in the hospital, we began telling people that Noah's time to live was short. Everyone who loved him came to say hello. Or goodbye. It seemed like a hundred people came to visit over the weekend. His face lit when his loud, younger sister, Tasha popped into his room. "Noah, I'm here!" she called. She'd been staying with her aunt and uncle so she could keep up with her middle-school classes while we lived at the hospital and cared for Noah.

Seeing her, his grandparents, godparents, relatives, teachers, friends from our neighborhood and his school gave him some energy, and that gave us hope. Noah seemed sheepish when three girls he'd had crushes on since kindergarten came to visit. Regina, Megan and Abby stood close to his bed, making small talk and later hugging and kissing him goodbye. They were seventeen, stylish, pretty and so healthy, and Noah was in his SpongeBob tee-shirt and pants that served as pajamas. Our parish priest, Father Mike, came and gave him Last Rites or, as it is called now, Anointing of the Sick. Noah took the oil on his forehead and chest stoically, saying "Amen" and crossing himself.

Noah was cheerful, so happy to be with his friends over those two days. He rallied and kept smiling, wide-awake and talking with visitors. Though he was still confined to his bed and on oxygen though a nose cone, people told us that he didn't seem that ill. We started to wonder—could we have misjudged? I wanted to believe the doctors were wrong and that he could pull through. I could believe in a miracle. After all, I'd prayed for one.

Mike and I relied on the wisdom of Pediatric Intensivist Dominic Sanfilippo, who oversaw Noah's care day-to-day. Pragmatic and compassionate, he had a warm and funny bedside manner. We sought him out on Monday morning after all the weekend visitors caused us to rethink Noah's prognosis. "Noah is doing so much better. He had a great weekend. He's really perked up," I said.

"He loved seeing his people and was sitting up in bed and talking with everyone," Mike said.

"I think he's doing better," I said.

"The reality is," the doctor said quietly shaking his head, "his breathing is becoming shallower and the carbon dioxide in his blood is increasing." He was direct, but not unkind in delivering the information from the chart in his hands. I gathered the courage and asked something that had been on my mind since Noah was admitted. "How long do you think he will live?" Tears glazed his brown eyes and he said, "He won't live long…maybe a few days at the most. Noah will decide when he is ready to leave."

The three of us stood outside the room with our backs turned away from Noah, but he saw us through the big glass window with a SpongeBob scene painted on it. "Dad. Mom. Come here!" He always seemed to know when we were talking about him. I couldn't go in the room and face him. Not yet. I needed time to gather myself. Throughout his hospital stay, I'd avoided letting Noah see me cry. So kind and sweet, he'd ask, "What's wrong, Mom? Please don't cry." This, of course, made me cry more. After a few deep breaths I went into his room and rested my head on his chest, my face turned away from his, and let his pajamas absorb my tears.

❖

I have no memory of putting the pen to paper, but I know we signed. I don't recall making my careless, cloud-like signature. Which one of us signed first? I may have pushed the Do Not Resuscitate papers toward Mike. It was what we both wanted for Noah. No, *wanted* isn't the right word: we didn't want Noah to die. We wanted him to live. We wanted him to come home from the hospital, recover from his lung infection and for our lives to return to what they were before he got sick. But what we wanted and the certainty of his prognosis weren't the same thing. The signing of the orders had to be done, so nothing would be done.

"This is where the nurses meet," I thought, as we were led into a plain room. One wall was covered by an oversized bulletin board tacked with personal notes, wage and hour regulations and a potluck announcement. Mike and I sat on one side of a long laminated table, a pediatric physician, chaplain and a social worker on the other side. Between us were a dull, faded flower arrangement and a few Martha Stewart magazines with the addresses cut off. We had talked through dozens of different scenarios before this meeting, weighing our options and questioning our decisions. What seemed like the right direction one hour would be wrong the next. Separate members of Noah's clinical team had talked with us about the orders during his hospitalization. Signing would make it official. The act of signing forced us to ask questions of ourselves and the clinical team about what was best for Noah and if there was any purpose in futile measures.

"If nothing is going to make him better or cure him, then why are we prolonging things?" I asked.

"Keeping Noah alive just to revive him doesn't make sense. I don't think the tubes, oxygen and suctioning are good for him," Mike said with a shaky voice. "It causes Noah too much pain. I hate seeing him in pain." He stared out the window for a long bit.

"He's suffering and I feel like we're just keeping him alive to let him die. That's not right," I said, looking directly the chaplain. I knew she was on our side.

"We understand," the doctor responded. I sighed and squeezed Mike's hand. Perhaps our wishes wouldn't be met with resistance or harsh questioning. I didn't know what to expect and wondered if there would be someone on staff who might be brought in to test our judgment or rationale. I bit my lip.

If Noah couldn't live like a normal seventeen-year-old, would his life be worth living? And Noah's *normal* was already complicated—because of his cerebral palsy, he used a wheelchair, needed ankle foot orthotics, wore arm splints, and had periodic Botox injections in his hands to loosen them up. He needed help with everything from schoolwork to getting dressed to taking showers. His daily care was a large part of our life as a family, and it was all any of us ever knew. We cared for him now in the same way we had when he was three, ten, or twelve years old.

The social worker began to speak, "Mike and Roberta are the parents of Noah, who has been in the PICU for three days. His prognosis is. . ."

What did she say? I don't remember. That his prognosis was grim? Grave? Fatal? I now realize that she didn't finish the sentence because had I buried my face on Mike's shoulder. The last thing I wanted to hear was this truth. Had I failed my son? I felt as if I had. All my good mothering wasn't going to keep my son alive. My head pounded. The team waited. When I lifted my head, she continued.

"Noah's parents have opted to sign *allow natural death* and *do not resuscitate* orders for their son. We want to make sure that they understand what we do in these situations," she said. The doctor explained the details.

We understood.

The orders would stop them from inserting a ventilator into Noah's lungs if he couldn't breathe on his own and it would avoid chest compressions if his heart stopped. *Allow natural death* orders would provide palliative care only, so our son would die comfortably. As much as we didn't want him to die, we wanted that.

Were we playing God? Hell, no. If I could have played God, I would have saved my son's life. But there was no saving Noah. He was too ill; his lungs were badly infected and scarred. He was too weak to cough, which was the one thing he could have done to help. We could have had him put on a ventilator every time he stopped breathing, but to what end? We were told that when the vent came out, it wouldn't be for long. Many parents take extreme measures to keep their children alive, but sometimes doing everything to save your child is too much.

Was it a selfish decision to allow him to die or was it compassionate and loving? We didn't want Noah to live breathlessly, in pain and fear. His green eyes showed terror as he gasped for air, his face was taut and his whole body tensed from the effort. It was painful for everyone.

We knew already that if he became well enough to be released from the hospital that he'd be too fragile to leave the house. Ever. How could we force our outgoing son to live within the confines of our home? All the things we did as a family, both ordinary and fun, would be prohibited. His life would be reduced to that of a sickly, bedridden child. That scared us as much as the thought of him dying.

We signed the orders with Noah's quality of life in mind, as well as our own. As parents and caregivers, his ongoing illness had become our illness, too. But we didn't want illness to be all that he owned. Noah deserved more. Life limited to a hospital or a house wasn't right for him or us, so we chose to let our son die. Ten days later, he was ready and we didn't interfere with his decision.

We never told Noah that he was going to die. We didn't tell him that we signed those papers, either. If he'd known we'd signed, he might have thought we didn't love him enough or weren't trying to do everything we could to keep him, and that just wasn't true.

❖

The weather that morning was bitterly cold with a sub-zero wind chill, though the sky was clear and sunny. Mike went to the PICU to be with Noah, and I went to the YMCA for a run. Running was my only release from stress. My friends Michael and Tommy were there. Coincidentally, I'd also had coffee with them the day Noah was admitted to the children's hospital, but I'd not seen or talked to them since. Unknowingly, they asked me what was going on—just a casual question—and I said, "Noah is going to die soon." It came out of my mouth so matter of fact, so easily, that I was instantly embarrassed. It was if Noah meant nothing to me and was as cruel as anything I'd ever spoken. Their faces went blank and they stopped talking, their shoulders fell and they looked at each other and the floor. One of them said, "I'm sorry." I felt cold and small. I questioned at that moment what I was doing away from the hospital. *What if* something was happening there without me? *What if* what I said to Michael and Tommy, that Noah was going to die soon, became reality? *What if* Noah was dying and I wasn't there? *What* kind of mother was I? Wandering off to the gym knowing my son could be dead when I returned to the hospital. I ran a few worried, distracted and guilty laps and stopped to call Mike.

"He's fine. Everything is the same," he said.

Back at Renucci House after my shower, I looked in the mirror and was taken aback at how old I looked. I felt old. My green eyes were permanently puffy, rimmed with red and dark circles; my inability to smile made me look drawn. I practiced smiling in the mirror. It looked and felt forced and painful. Smiling felt wrong, like something I wasn't supposed to do anymore.

Back at the hospital, I called my friend Jane in a panic, the reality of what was happening was settling more deeply in my mind. I felt chilled and my heart was thumping in my chest. Jane was the one I called for help because she knew what to do.

"Jane, the doctor doesn't think Noah has long to live. Maybe just a few days. It doesn't look good."

"I'll be there as soon as I'm able," she said. "I'll have Greg call Father Mike and have a hospital lay minister come by to see you." She and her husband Greg were Noah's godparents.

Mike and I sat in Noah's room lost in our personal thoughts with little to say. We'd heard the news, wept with his doctor, and now Mike and I were silenced. We looked back and forth at one another over Noah's bed trying not to make him think anything was unusual.

"I'm going to take a walk," Mike said.

"I'll be here." I stood up, went to Noah's bed and messed with his hair.

A few minutes passed when an older lady in a robin's egg blue cardigan, khakis and clean white sneakers appeared at the door. She leaned in.

"I'm here to offer the Eucharist," she said.

I nodded and stood up to welcome her. She made the sign of the cross on Noah's forehead and chest and asked if he could take communion. "Yes," I whispered. Noah opened his mouth and the lay minister fed him. I took his hand and helped him make the sign of the cross. I held out my palm to the woman.

"The body of Christ," she said, placing the wafer in my palm.

"Amen," I replied as she snapped the portable communion case shut. She said a quiet prayer, placed a rosary in Noah's hand, and left the room.

I felt tired and sank into the recliner next to the bed. I wish I'd felt the brush of angel's wings or something spiritually significant, even a hint of calm, but I didn't. I didn't feel much of anything. Noah was resting with his eyes closed, and he looked peaceful, which was a good sign. The oxygen cone on his nose kept him breathing easily and his pale face had a tinge of pink on the cheeks. He slept and I kissed him.

When Jane finally came by, it was just after lunch. She was between work meetings and could only stay for a bit. Mike and I were just back from a fast dash to the cafeteria. The whole lunch was spent worrying about Noah and sorting out the possibility that he might come home to die. We were expecting a visit from a hospice nurse to help us decide how his last days might play out. "I'd just rather have him die in the house," I said. "After all, you practically built that house for him."

"It would be better than dying here, I guess," Mike said looking around. "But won't that be strange, maybe, to have him die, like right in the living room? What do you think that's going to be like?"

"I don't know. I never thought about it… where it might happen," I said. I imagined, though, that he would die in his own twin bed, not in a rented hospital bed. Clearly, we hadn't really thought this through. The logistics of turning our home into a place for Noah's peaceful death were details for which we had no context or experience. It just seemed like the right thing to do, rather than settle for an in-hospital death. We didn't have the mental material for a deep conversation; it was just too hard to figure out. We knew for certain that we wanted to try to bring him home, if possible. In the end, though, Noah died more suddenly than we expected and we weren't able to bring him home.

Other than the lay minister and Mike's sister Janice, Jane was our only visitor the day of his death. She and I talked about his illness and what the doctor had told us that morning. She rubbed Noah's head and held his hand while we talked. When the nurse from Harbor Hospice arrived, Jane left for a meeting and Janice stayed with Noah.

We kissed him before we left the room telling him we'd be close by.

"Noah, we're talking to someone about bringing you home," I told him. "Aunt Janice will be here with you."

"We'll be right around the corner if you need us," Mike said. Noah smiled and blew us a kiss in return. He didn't say anything.

Just moments later, Janice ran into the conference room to get us. "Hurry, come quick! Noah's in trouble," she said. Her voice was pinched; her face was pale with eyes large from fear. When we got there, his room was crowded with hospital staff, anxiously working on him, adjusting his oxygen and changing the mask.

Noah had made his decision. We could not keep death away any longer. Mike told the staff to let him go. "Stop. No more. He's had enough. Let him be." Janice and the hospital staff backed away from his bed—observing instead of working. The room became absolutely still and quiet.

We talked Noah to the other side and comforted him as best we could. Taking another human being, especially your own child, from life to death is mysterious and powerful. It created an indelible memory that remains forever fresh in my mind. The words I spoke as he went from this life to the next were from the core of my being, from my heart and perhaps even my soul. I won't ever forget what I said.

"Don't be afraid Noah. It'll be good in heaven, love. You'll be able to breathe again," I told him. I thought he might like to know that because his labored breathing and coughing bothered him. "We're here with you right now, and we'll be with you always. Don't be scared."

"Grandma King will be waiting for you in heaven and Grandpa Miesch. Remember my friend Jeff? They'll all be looking for you, Noah," I said. "Jesus and Mary will take care of you, too. It will be okay, love, I promise." I wanted him to know that he would not be alone for long. He became pale, and the pink of his cheeks and lips began to fade to white. His eyelids fluttered occasionally, but his eyes were mostly closed.

"I'm sorry," I said. I don't know why I said that. I felt sorry for myself that he was leaving.

I could hear Mike telling Noah how much he loved him and not to be afraid.

"Be brave, Noah," he said. "I know you will. There's nothing to be scared of. We're here for you. I'll love you always."

"I'll miss you Noah. I'll miss you all the time, every day. I know I will. I love you," I said, repeating it over and over. We wanted to make sure he knew this one thing, without a single doubt.

We told him not be afraid of what was happening, though we didn't really know anything for certain ourselves. Noah was fearless; he went bravely and without hesitation to death. He looked thoughtful and his brow was furrowed. When he gasped and struggled to breathe, I panicked. I called out to the nurse to help him; I didn't want him to suffer. "Help him. He's in pain! Give him something." I said.

"He's not suffering. It's okay," she said. "This is just how people die. There's often a little struggle, some resistance. He's doing fine." I had to trust her. I put my cheek on his and whispered words of love and reassurance. I rubbed his head, feeling the spring of his curly hair. I kissed his hands, which were cool, relaxed and soft. I could hear Mike whispering to our son over and again, "I love you, Noah. I love you. It'll be okay."

As Noah journeyed forward to his death, Mike and I held tightly onto each other and to him. Finally, as he drew his last troubled breath, we let the most amazing kid we'd ever known go where he wanted to go. Home.

❖

We stood next to his bed taking in what we had just seen and done. We barely spoke. We had experienced a miracle of sorts, and we were awestruck. Parents are given a gift when they bring their child into this world. Some parents, like Mike and me, are given something else, not quite a gift, but the deeply spiritual and personal experience of guiding a child out of this life. I finally felt the adrenaline that had been coursing through my body slowly start to diminish with February's bleak light. I looked around the room, not sure what to do next. For an hour or so after Noah died, Mike and I stayed with him, touching his hair, holding his hands, looking at his face, kissing his cheeks and crying. We noticed how a small scratch near his mouth had disappeared and how his hands, normally stiff from the cerebral palsy were completely relaxed. I kissed them and sniffed them for the last time. Though his hands were often cold, the coolness that now took over his body felt different. His skin seemed drier than usual. We'd just taken our lovely son to the other side and now we were seeing his body for the very last time. I didn't want to leave him and resisted even looking away. I didn't want to leave him because I knew I'd never see him again after that day.

The hospital staff offered to give him a bath and take the oxygen support and other monitors from the room while we phoned family members. They told us we could stay with Noah as long as we wished, and if people wanted to come to his room, they were welcome. As reluctant as we were to leave him, even for a bit, we needed to call his grandfather, sister and other family members with the news.

"I'll make the call to the funeral home for you," the hospice nurse offered.

"Sytsema in Muskegon," I said. "Tell them to send Dan. It can't be anyone else. It has to be Dan." We were never more grateful to have a friend in the funeral business than we were that day. My mother died several years before Noah. She and my dad had pre-arranged their funerals and a strange man I'd never met handled hers. He didn't know us or my mom. His desire to remove details from her obituary (to save money, I suppose) rankled me. I purposefully argued with him as we made plans. It was unpleasant, sad and irritating.

We'd known Dan most of our married life. We bought his old yellow house in 1988, and it was newborn Noah's first home. I can't imagine what it might have felt like to give Noah's body over to someone we didn't know. During his life we handed him over to caring strangers—when he went to daycare, camp, or school—but that was different. On this day it had to be someone who knew us and knew Noah. Dan provided security and solace.

The hospice nurse returned to Noah's room. "Dan was sorry to hear about Noah's death," she said. "He's ready to come over whenever you need him. The staff just needs to call."

We were guided to a small room with overstuffed chairs, a low-lit lamp and a corner table with a box of tissues as a centerpiece. A large print of a meadow done in subtle yellows, greens, and browns was positioned at eye-level to provide calm and serenity. I looked at the artwork and the room and thought, "Bad news is delivered here."

We already had our bad news. In our presence, and on his own terms, Noah followed a short path over two weeks from sick child to dead son.

"I better call my dad," I said. My hands were shaking, and I was relieved that my mobile phone had important numbers programmed in. At least something would be easy.

"Hi. It's me," I said as my dad picked up the phone.

How does a daughter tell her father that his only grandson is dead? Are there any right words to deliver comfort and terrible news at the same time? I felt like I needed to do both.

"Hi, it's me. I'm sorry to tell you, but Noah died." I squeaked out that much.

"Oh dear," he said. "When did it happen?"

"Just a little while ago, around three. He just couldn't breathe anymore," I said.

"Do you want me to come to the hospital? Do you need anything?"

"Yes, you and Uncle Dick should come over, and please hurry. No, I don't think we need anything, just you," I said. "I love you, too." I pressed End.

"I should call my mom," Mike said. He dialed and I turned away. I wasn't used to seeing him cry, and it made me feel even more vulnerable.

We continued making calls, trading off the responsibility of who had to speak to whom. Tasha was staying with her aunt and uncle and I wanted to have her at the hospital, to tell her the news in person. She knew Noah was sick, though she didn't know he was going to die.

"Kathy, it's me," I whispered in the phone. I didn't need to whisper, but I thought the timing was such that she might have picked Tasha up at school and was possibly on the way home.

"Noah died a little while ago," I said. "Would you bring Tasha to the hospital, please? Thank you. Sure, put her on." I could hear a bit of their muffled conversation over the sounds of the road and car radio. I thought about Kathy, who'd taken Noah for weekends and cared for him, how she was now driving, knowing her nephew was dead and not being able to react to the news to protect her niece. Her half hour drive to the hospital wouldn't be easy.

"Hi Tasha!" I said with false cheeriness, trying to hide the pinch, tightness and waver in my voice.

"Aunt Kathy says we're coming up to the hospital," she said. "I can't wait to see Noah."

"Oh, honey. We'll see you soon. Bye-bye," I said, disconnecting before I had to say anything else.

"Tasha is on her way here," I said. "What are we going to do?"

"You've got to tell her," Mike said.

"I know that," I said, trying not to be annoyed. "But what do we say? When? She's going to fall apart. She didn't see this coming."

"This is going to be bad. We should have probably told her more than we did. I wish we'd just told her the truth." Maybe she didn't need the protection I wanted to give her. Perhaps more preparation would have been less cruel.

We held each other tight. Mike's fleece sweatshirt was soft and I used it to wipe my eyes. I could feel his ragged breathing and thumping heart. I knew he was crying again, too.

"I love you," he said.

"Love you, too. God, I'm missing Noah so much," I said.

"I can't imagine life without him," he said.

"Me, either. The idea of going home without him scares me. What will we do without him? The house won't be the same, nothing will be the same," I said. All the change we were facing seemed vast and overpowering.

"I don't know… I just don't know."

"I can't believe he's dead," I said. This is something I said over and over that afternoon and evening, and even years later, I am in disbelief. Still.

❖

Tasha was Noah's sister for just five years. She came to us at age eight as a foster child and we adopted her a year later. Her "pre-us" life had been terrible and rough. Abuse heaped on top of neglect left her damaged and depleted—mentally, physically and emotionally. But Noah gave her something she never had— unconditional love. She was his protector, defender, helper and best friend. They spent hours each day together messing around, playing games, watching videos, or taking wheelchair walks with her happily pushing. It wasn't always easy—they'd fight and call names—but it was clear she loved him more than she loved anyone else. Noah didn't make demands on her like adults did, and that made him perfect in her mind.

We knew his death was going to be difficult for her, so over the past weeks we had withheld information about how serious his condition was. Partially, I didn't want to deal with her emotional distress. I had enough of my own anxiety and pre-grief sadness, and adding her into the mix didn't seem like a good thing for anyone. Now we were going to have to find a way to break this news to her.

Strategically stationed in the hall outside the PICU, we waited. If we weren't in the hall to stop Tasha, she'd run into the hospital room where Noah's body lay.

"Mom! Dad! I want to go see Noah," she cried as she burst off the elevator wearing a lime-colored ski jacket. Her wet snow boots squeaked on the waxed floor. Her long, thick brown hair was in a ponytail and her brown eyes were full of anticipation. Kathy followed, her face red, puffy and stressed. Mike's brother Chuck followed behind them, looking down as we all met.

"Hey. Hold on. How about a hug for me?" I said, trying to slow Tasha down.

She gave me a quick hug. "I want to go see Noah." It had only been two days since her last hospital visit, but for her twelve-year-old heart it must have seemed much longer.

"Wait. Wait. Let's talk a sec," Mike said.

"Come here," I said grabbing her hand, leading her into the bad news room. Mike closed the door and leaned against it. "Sit down, Tasha."

Her face lost its excitement as she sat down. She already knew we had something bad to say. She tossed her jacket on a chair.

"Where's Noah? Why won't you let me see Noah?" she begged.

"Honey," I said, as I tried to think of words that would make sense to her. This was her first death experience. "This is going to be hard for you to understand or believe, but Noah died this afternoon," I said as calmly as I could, trying not to cry myself.

She jumped up as if she'd had an electrical shock. She leaped toward the door and Mike.

"No!" she screamed. "What happened? Why did Noah die? What do you mean? No."

"He just died, Tasha, that's all. He was ready to go. He was having a hard time breathing and couldn't hang on anymore. Dad and I were with him."

"Where is he?" Her face was wet with tears and her fists were clenched.

"He's in heaven now," I said.

"No! Not already! I want to see him. Oh no," she panicked, flinging herself into a chair face first. "Noah!"

"Oh my, Tasha. I'm sorry. I said that wrong. You can still see Noah. His body is still here. I thought you meant..." I didn't bother to finish.

She pushed Mike away, or tried to.

"Give me your hand, Tasha. Let's go down and see him together," I said, and we walked down the hall together.

"Mom. Why did Noah die?"

"He just had to. He was too sick and couldn't breathe anymore. It was too hard for him to keep living." I would repeat this to her over and again for the next few days. I wished I had better answers, something that made more sense.

She went straight to him, crying and whispering things I couldn't understand. She took his now-cool hand and pressed it to her face. She wasn't afraid or aware of the social mores regarding bodies of the dead. She hugged him and climbed onto the hospital bed next to him, as if they were just resting together.

"I love you, Noah," she said softly into his ear.

That afternoon we shared Tasha's deep sadness. As moments passed into hours and the sky grew dusky, the reality of our loss was magnified by the grief of family and friends who came to see Noah and us. Noah lay in the hospital bed, dressed for the last time in the SpongeBob t-shirt and pajama bottoms, tucked in with a blanket. He had a little ring on his finger that I bought for him up north the summer before. I wrapped a rosary lightly around one hand. He smelled clean and his hair was damp, and very curly. His left ear had a gold stud earring in it. We'd had it pierced when he was six and he always wore an earring.

He didn't look dead to me… or maybe I didn't know what a dead child looked like.

The closed curtains between Noah's room and the hall would be the only difference anyone might notice as different from visiting another sick kid on the PICU. Most of the time the curtains were open, so nurses could keep an eye on their patients. As we sat with Noah, Mike opened the curtains in Noah's room. That evening's sunset was a blaze of orange, pink and blue, with layers of thin cirrus clouds. It glowed down a corridor from big west-facing window.

"Noah would like the sky tonight," he said.

"Yes, he would," I replied, as we both looked at the colorful sky.

"But people coming to visit the other kids probably wouldn't want to see a dead child in a room."

He closed the curtains.

It was dark outside now, and we needed to go home. The hospital staff called Dan to come for Noah. While we waited, I clipped a few locks of Noah's blonde curls as a keepsake. Jodi, the child-life specialist stopped by and commandeered Tasha, taking her away and occupying her with snacks, games and puzzles while we lingered at Noah's bedside. Dan appeared at the doorway, wearing a long, black wool coat and a scarf. He stood over six feet tall, lanky, with bright blue eyes and spiky blonde hair. Normally he looked a bit like a rock and roll musician, but the clothing and expression he wore this night made him look like a funeral director. He looked solemn and spoke with quiet resolve, almost with caution. We gathered around Noah. I don't know if Dan was unusually quiet because it was his job or because it was Noah.

"I'll take Noah's body back to Muskegon, and in the morning, we can meet and make funeral plans. Think about what you'd like in an obituary and bring a photograph you like," he said.

We never saw a body bag or even the stretcher they took him away on. We walked slowly down the hall out of the hospital, leaving Noah in Dan's care.

Life Stories

May you live all the days of your life.
—Jonathan Swift

chapter 2 | Birth Day

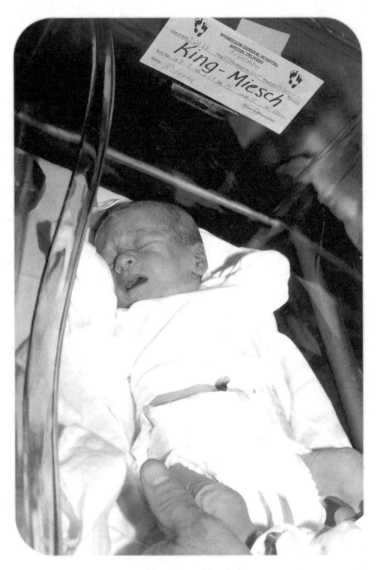

Newborn Noah.

"Hello, Love."

Noah blinked his dark eyes.

I'd planned to say "Hello, Love" for months before Noah was born. I wanted my first words to him to be memorable. They would become part of a story to tell him as he grew up. While pregnant, I daydreamed that on his birthday each year, we'd go out for lunch and he'd say, "Mom, tell me about the day I was born." And I'd say, "The first words I ever spoke to you were, 'Hello, Love.'"

So I chose the simple words from the Garrison Keillor song that opened *Prairie Home Companion* each week. I wanted to sing a line or two from the song, but the anesthesia from the emergency C-section scrambled my mind. Noah decided to arrive a month before his due date. He weighed just four pounds, nine ounces.

❖

Less than an hour before Noah's birth, Mike traipsed into the operating room wearing surgical scrubs. Dr. Karnes and I were waiting; he was keeping an eye on Noah's intrauterine vitals, which were weak. Time was running out and the delivery needed to begin.

"There's a toilet paper tail on your foot," I said to Mike.

He looked down and used his other foot to remove it. We laughed, nervously.

"Sit right there, Mike," the doctor said, pointing to a wheeled stool near my head.

Prior to that morning, there wasn't any indication that anything was amiss with the pregnancy. While I was writing thank you notes from a baby shower, I felt something like contractions or what I'd heard or read might be contractions. It was the timing that concerned me. They were to the second, ten minutes apart. These tiny contractions continued for an hour until I picked up the phone. Dr. Karnes told me to come to the hospital immediately.

Time compressed, expanded and mashed up from incision to birth, like a time-lapse film. I faded in and out under the anesthesia as people came and went from the operating room and recovery rooms. I heard Mike, Dr. Karnes and the nurses. I didn't know which room I was in or where Noah was. It might have been a few minutes or a few hours.

❖

Noah was sleeping on my chest, my head and shoulders propped up with two pillows so I could see this brand new tiny boy. He was wrinkled and darker than I'd expected. His hands were clenched up near his head. There wasn't a sign of the blonde curls that would become one of his most distinguishing features—just a few wisps of light brown hair. I rested my cheek on the top of his head. It was warm and sweet smelling and tangy, like yogurt. He looked a little troubled; his forehead had a crease of concern.

"Don't worry, Noah," I whispered.

I would worry for him and about him, this tiny sweet creature, so new to the world, so new to us.

I tried to think of something more comforting to say—but could not—so I kissed him instead.

chapter 3 | Reading Aloud

Noah with books on sofa.

When I learned I was going to be a mother, I started building Noah's personal library. I planned to make him into a good reader by surrounding him with books and reading aloud to him every day.

When I was young, reading *The Bobbsey Twins* series, *Charlotte's Web, Little House on the Prairie, Harriet the Spy* and *Nancy Drew* introduced me to people who were more interesting than the kids at school or across the street. I felt kinship with people in books. They were more than characters, and I often imagined myself playing with Nan and Bert or spying with Harriet. I longed to be a twin or a motherless mystery solver. I dreamed of living in New York City or in a desolate northern wood with a blind sister. Any life seemed more interesting than my ordinary middle-class upbringing. However, I knew the reality of farm life, like that of Fern, Wilbur, and Charlotte. Weeklong summer visits with my five cousins, who lived on a mid-Michigan soybean farm, cured me of farm envy. Nevertheless, all of these stories told me about things I'd never experienced. I was determined that my son would follow the same path of bookish love and live for those kind of adventures we would read about.

From my personal collection, I handed down to him *The World of Pooh,* a thick hardcover with a torn dust jacket that my parents had read to me. Wonderful watercolor illustrations, and simple pen and ink drawings were sprinkled on the pages. I stocked Noah's shelves with *Goodnight Moon, Curious George, Where the Wild Things Are,* miniature volumes of Beatrix Potter and Ezra Jack Keats' *A Snowy Day.* I bought books for reading to a newborn, toddler and preschooler. Noah would be a great reader one day, ensured by an extensive home library.

❖

Reading wasn't much on my mind on a warm October morning, as I made my daily trip to the hospital to visit my son. He'd been there for twenty days. He was fragile at first, but there were no major complications or concerns. The day when the neonatal pediatrician told me he could go home, Noah weighed just five pounds, which was the weight he needed to reach to be discharged. I'd work hard to get him to his weight by nursing, pumping and praying that he'd meet this milestone.

"Really? Just like that? He can come home this afternoon?" I asked. He was such a tiny fragile human; the hospital felt safer than home. The nurses knew more than I did about mothering, and I liked their advice and help.

"You can take him home now. I'm getting the discharge papers in order," he replied.

I hesitated. I was alone. Mike was at work. What was I going to do with a baby for the rest of the day? I'd fallen into a routine of coming up to the hospital each morning, sitting in a comfy rocker in the nursery with the other babies and nursing staff. I'd breastfeed and hold Noah until the afternoon, daydreaming and reading my manifesto, *The Womanly Art of Breastfeeding*. After the second shift nurses settled in, I'd head home to make dinner, and later Mike and I would return to the hospital, feeding, holding and reading to Noah before going home again to sleep.

I wanted to wait a few more hours before leaving that morning. I suspected, though, it would reflect poorly upon me if I didn't seem eager to bring my newborn home. I packed my bundled baby into a car seat and said goodbye to the nurses as we were officially discharged. I drove away with Noah in my blue

Toyota Tercel. I pulled over twice during the five-mile drive home to check on him. There wasn't anything wrong with him—other than being so small—I just worried that he might stop breathing. A preemie baby wasn't anything we expected, and his vulnerability scared me.

I carefully placed the car seat with baby on our big wooden porch as I unlocked the front door.

Nicky, a neighbor kid, dropped his football in his yard and walked up the porch steps, to peer at Noah. "He looks like a gerbil," he said. "What's his name?"

"Get off my porch, you little shit!" I was edgy and hormonal. His comment heightened my anxiety.

As he hurried back to his yard, I called somewhat apologetically, "His name is Noah!"

I extricated my tiny son from the multiple seat straps and settled him safely on the sofa. Our collie, Franny, ambled up for a sniff.

"Get away from my baby," I snapped. The dog slunk off to its bed and lay down with a sigh. A puff of dog hair and dust twinkled in the sunlight, landed and skated across the wooden floor.

Things were different now.

Noah napped as I put away the preemie diapers and some tiny undershirts from the hospital, wondering what to do next. It wasn't even 11 a.m. when I called my parents' house. My mom was teaching until 3:30, but my dad was retired. He had nothing but time on his hands. "I'll try to come over when I'm done mowing the lawn," he said. I felt like something more ought to be happening, but nothing was.

I rearranged things in Noah's nursery and got the changing table set for action. He'd eventually wake up and pee, and I would change his diaper.

We sat in the Sleepy Hollow chair next to the bookshelf and he slept in the crook of my arm. He was tiny and wrinkled, his little hands were up around his face, kind of like…a gerbil. I had brought a few books down from his nursery—a board book about colors with photographs of babies, *Dr. Seuss' ABC* book and just in case, *Charlotte's Web*. I didn't know what he'd like to hear, and I was prepared to read anything he might respond to—colorful or rhyme-y—I wanted to please him.

I read to Noah throughout each day during my maternity leave. Every evening before he went to sleep, we'd read through a half dozen books, maybe more—depending on content and depth. I'd point out interesting features of the illustrations and ask him questions.

"Look at this baby here, does she look sad or happy? Do you see her blue umbrella?"

"Do you think Pooh will be able to get out of that hole? He's very stuck."

Noah would blink. Reading to an infant is like reading aloud. Alone.

❖

As a toddler, he'd sit on the sofa or lie on the floor and leaf through the books we provided. He loved the shape and color board books with photographs of babies and children in them and would ask for specific books by name, "Pool book," he'd say for *McElligot's Pool* or "Pancakes" for *Curious George Makes Pancakes*. His requests for specific books gave me hope. Perhaps my early intervention had worked, though the physical delays from cerebral palsy were starting to show, intellectually he seemed to be making progress.

By first grade, reading wasn't going well for Noah. Despite his teacher's efforts, nightly home reading sessions and my now retired-teacher-mom's tutoring, he wasn't making progress like other kids his age. He could sight read some words and would finish sentences from books I was reading to him. I'd start a page from *Chicken Soup with Rice* and stop reading, and he'd finish it word for word, page after page from memory. It felt like real reading was just around the corner. As time passed I read progressively more complex books for his age. When he was in the second and third grade, I was still doing most of the reading. He could pick out a word here or there, could sometimes put two words together, but reading was coming very slowly. I cried when Noah's fourth grade teacher told me he'd never be able to read. I had been holding out hope for nine years that one day the concept of reading would click.

"He just doesn't have the capacity to learn to read. We will always keep trying, but we need to focus on other things he can do," she said.

I wiped my eyes, bit my bottom lip, looked at some papers on the desk, and tried not to appear too disappointed. She was surprised at my reaction and shook her head. Obviously she didn't know how hopeful (and naïve) I was about reading. Maybe she just didn't know how badly I'd wanted this one thing to be his, ours to share. "I just don't think it will happen. I'm sorry," she said.

She was right. Noah never learned to read. He never learned to do math, science or geography either. His cerebral palsy that came with his premature birth went beyond the physical, and affected his ability to learn. His verbal skills were limited too. He spoke only in simple sentences, asked basic questions and presented rudimentary ideas in our conversations.

By medical definition, he had severe cognitive and physical impairments, but he never felt that way to us. It even feels odd for me to write these words now because all we saw in Noah was intelligence, keen observation skills, personal charm and a fine sense of humor. The emotional disappointment of disability nibbled at me throughout his life; it was bothersome, but never overwhelming. Certainly, I felt a sense of loss and sadness, because no matter what anyone says, kids with disabilities have both societal and personal constraints in their lives that present large, and sometimes overwhelming, challenges. His disability was never about giving up on our expectations for his life; it was about changing those expectations and learning as he grew that his life wouldn't be ordinary. My pragmatic side didn't allow for whining, wishing or wondering about how this might play out in the future. We couldn't change Noah or fix what wasn't quite right so we flexed our life around him and what he could do.

Noah was never able to stand, walk or run. He used a wheelchair starting just before kindergarten. His clenched and shaky hands made it difficult and awkward for him to feed himself or color on a page, and he wore splints on his lower arms to keep them from bending downward. He chose his clothes, but we dressed him each day and put him on the toilet. He was totally dependent on his dad and me for his care.

I knew, though, that books and reading would open to him a world far beyond what we could offer. Though we could provide much for him, there were adventures he could never have without the help of books. So, I forged on—reading aloud to him into his seventeenth year—always holding onto to a thread of hope that *my* reading might magically turn into *his* reading. I read *Toad and Frog* and *Little Bear* and *The BFG* and the *Phantom Toll Booth*. I read *The Stinky Cheese Man* at least twenty times and read *The Wizard of Oz* from the Illustrated Junior Classics series. *The Great Brain* and *Charlie and the Chocolate Factory*. Age appropriate books bought from Scholastic, school fairs and stores. We borrowed from the library and immersed ourselves in reading. Noah never did learn to read, but he knew his books.

One day at the bookstore, he spotted J. K. Rowling's *Harry Potter and the Sorcerer's Stone*.

"Let's read Harry Potter," he said.

I picked it up. It was a heavy hardcover with small print and 309 pages.

"Everyone is reading Harry Potter," he said. "I want to read Harry Potter."

It took me six months to read it to him. I stood beside Noah's bed, or rested on the edge of it each night and plodded through. He liked it even though I found it awkward to read aloud. The British-isms and word play that flowed naturally in silent reading caused me to overthink and hesitate, rather than read aloud with confidence.

"What kind of name is Hermione? I've never heard of such a name," I said to myself. "How is it pronounced?" It caused me to stumble, so I substituted Heather for the smart, cute girl. Noah was shocked when we went to the Harry Potter movie a few years later.

"Hermione?" he blurted in disbelief. "I thought she was Heather."

"Shh. Watch the movie and don't talk," I whispered back.

One night, as I took *Harry Potter and the Sorcerer's Stone* from the nightstand to work through another few pages, Noah asked, "Can we read something else?"

"Don't you like Harry Potter?"

"Yes… but it's complicated."

"I agree. All that wizardy stuff is complicated. Let's find something else for tonight," I said.

I looked at the choices and pulled *Charlotte's Web* from the shelf. Instead of sitting, I moved Noah over closer to the wall and lay down next to him in his twin bed. I could feel his breath in my ear. I read my favorite chapter, "Escape," where Wilbur finds a loose board in the barnyard fence, runs out and experiences freedom for a short while. He only returns to the pen enticed by a pail of warm slops and the reassuring voice of the still-kind Homer Zuckerman.

That sweet story of time outside the pen with Wilbur's frolicking escape seemed less complicated and we both laughed as I read it. In our life, less complication, even when temporary, was something we cherished.

CHAPTER 4 | Blame it on Harry

Noah in his OshKosh bibs.

There's no way Noah could have done it. I know Mike or I would have noticed such a thing, so we just blame it on Harry Houdini.

When Noah was three years old, we went across Lake Michigan on the S.S. Badger, an old coal-burning cross-lake ferry that travels from Ludington, Michigan, to Manitowoc, Wisconsin. It was just the three of us, and oddly, neither Mike nor I can recall this trip's reason or our final destination. We put our car on the ferry and moved Noah up deck from his car seat to a specialized stroller. This was a pre-wheelchair time of our lives, and Noah had a light blue, heavy-duty foldable stroller that could brutally pinch a finger in the unfolding. We had that stroller until Noah got his first wheelchair just before he started school.

Noah's physical issues became obvious when he was around six months old. He wasn't sitting up on his own or rolling around on the floor as the child-rearing books said he should be. I attributed it to his premature birth and expected he'd eventually catch up. The summer before he was one year old, we were at a friend's cottage and as always, we carried him around and sat him on our laps or in chairs.

"Just put him there in the sand," said my friend's mother. "He can play with the toys," she said pointing to a shaded area, not too close to the water.

"He usually falls over," I said. "But I'll try." She was trying to be helpful to a new mom—that's all. I carefully placed Noah in the sand, molding his diapered bottom to the ground, building a little hill behind him for support. I tentatively stepped back and within a few seconds, he fell over, the back of his head and shoulders gently hitting the sand. We tried again. He wasn't crying, but he wasn't sitting up either.

"How old is he?" my friend's mother asked.

"Ten months."

"Something isn't right," she said. "He should be able to sit up." I knew what she was saying was true, but he seemed to be thriving in other ways; he was a good eater, very social and outgoing, slept well and was babbling like babies do. He looked perfectly normal—cute and sweet, and we were first-time parents. Perhaps we should have taken Noah to a pediatrician instead of a family physician since his birth was early and he was tiny. It's easy now to question decisions made or not made.

When Noah was two years old we began to observe that his right foot and lower leg were gently kicking involuntarily. It was like the limb was nervous or restless. People do this sometimes with a leg or foot, a rapid pulsing or tapping that they don't often notice. The family physician sent us to see a neurologist in Muskegon and that day we began what would be a multi-year foray into pediatric medicine with its specialties and subspecialties—searching for answers.

"I can do a few tests and I see kids in this practice, but he's pretty young. I'd like to refer him to one of my professors from the University of Michigan," said the local neurologist. We took Noah to C.S. Mott Children's Hospital in Ann Arbor. At sixteen months old, he wasn't hitting the physical milestones of even a nine-month-old baby.

"Well, cerebral palsy is a junk bin for all sorts of things. When doctors can't specifically determine the cause of a neurological condition we call it cerebral palsy," the pediatric neurologist said.

"I'd like to try to find out more about Noah and the cause of his condition," he said as he delved into details about my pregnancy, Noah's delivery and his progress so far.

"Will he get worse?" I asked.

"Not likely. CP is static. It is what it is. It isn't degenerative. It will change somewhat as he grows, though," he said. "You'll see differences over time in how his body reacts."

This was a whole new page in the baby book for us.

"That's good? Right?" said Mike.

"Well, yes, for now. From what we know he shouldn't get any worse and we can do some things to help him grow stronger," the doctor said.

He asked his nurse to schedule some tests—an MRI, blood work, an EEG and others. He sent us home with a prescription for some pills that made the shaking foot go away but left Noah limp, weak and drooling. We quit that medicine and let his foot carry on with its trembling. We read the brochures provided and found a few books at the library on cerebral palsy, but there was no child in the case studies with symptoms just like Noah's.

After almost three years of tests, the old doctor's retirement and working with a new young pediatric neurologist, we cried *uncle* and gave up trying to find out exactly what Noah had. He'd been examined, sedated, PET scanned, MRI'd, prodded, injected, poked, biopsied, drugged, weaned off drugs enough times to satisfy us. It felt to us like there were no answers to be found.

"It really doesn't matter anymore what the cause was or what it is," Mike said. "If he's not going to get worse, then why are we doing all this testing?"

The new neurologist agreed.

"Sometimes we never find out what went wrong or exactly what a patient has. Let's check in every year. If you see anything new happening or something changes before then, let me know. We can always continue to try to land on a diagnosis," she said.

Mike and I drove home from Ann Arbor and returned there only one more time while Noah was very young. Noah seemed healthy and happy—nothing appeared to be changing. We structured our lives around his disability and accepted that difference would be our kind of normal. Wheelchairs became part of that normal. So did hand splints, braces, ankle-foot orthotics (AFOs) and a wide range of devices intended to support and prop Noah, to keep his body from doing what it wanted to do instead of what it was supposed to do.

❖

It's odd to think of travel planned without the internet, GPS devices and MapQuest but this was 1991 so we went to AAA for a map and a guidebook and used the phone for trip planning. We were ready to start our son on travel adventures, and the trip to Manitowoc, Wisconsin, would be his first across Lake Michigan. The boat docked at noon in Manitowoc, and we planned to drive an hour to Appleton after lunch. But first we had to find lunch. Indecision in choosing a place to eat has always been problematic in travel. I'm a vegetarian and Mike is a beeratarian. That is, he likes a beer with lunch or dinner or even in between. We drove around Manitowoc and finally found a bar that had grilled cheese sandwiches and a decent beer selection.

From what we'd read about Appleton, the town didn't offer much except a Harry Houdini Museum, which closed at 4 p.m. and a brewpub that we wanted to hit for dinner. It was just a waypoint to break up a travel day.

"We're going to a Houdini Museum, Noah," I told him. At age three he didn't understand this, but as parents who believed in a far-ranging cultural education, we felt it important we expose him to a wide variety of activities and experiences. "Harry Houdini lived in Appleton and was a very famous escape artist. He could be tied up in ropes or chains or locked in a box and could always escape. He was very clever and very flexible," I said. That was about all I knew about Houdini.

Road construction delayed our travel, so by the time we got to Appleton it was late. Also, I'd spotted an outlet mall with an OshKosh store on the way and made Mike stop. I adored how Noah looked in OshKosh bib overalls. They were great pants for a skinny kid, with adjustable shoulder straps there were no issues with keeping things up around his waist. As I shopped, Mike waited outside in the summer sun. Neither he nor Noah was interested in this kind of shopping—any kind of shopping really. As I was checking out, Mike mentioned that I'd squandered almost an hour in the store. "I don't know if we'll have time to see the Houdini Museum," he said.

"Sure doesn't look like it. Maybe we'll have to pass. Maybe we can go there tomorrow before we head out of town," I said. Noah didn't seem perturbed by the change of plans. "Hey Noah, there's a pool at the hotel, we'll go swimming. That sounds like more fun than a Houdini Museum doesn't it?"

"I want to swim," he said.

That afternoon we drove around Appleton, walked in its pretty downtown and swam at the hotel. For dinner we found the brewpub, the AdlerBrau. It was an oddly located place, in a renovated brewery bottling plant-now-a-mall space. It was dark and cozy with stonewalls and a cave-like feel. We'd read about it in a Midwest beer magazine, and it probably had a lot to do with us stopping in Appleton in the first place. We liked the beer so much that we bought a couple of six packs to go.

"We need to get some ice in the cooler," Mike said as we left the pub. He arranged the stroller in the back of our station wagon, and I locked Noah into his car seat. He'd moved up from the baby "bucket" seat and was in a toddler seat that had an over-the-head and shoulder harness that buckled between his legs. Summer was a time of caution: more than once I'd pinched his tender thigh in the crotch buckle.

We drove to a gas station and Mike went in for ice. I sat in the car and talked with Noah and listened to music on a cassette tape. It seemed like it was taking a long time to get the ice.

"Gee, Noah. Wonder what your dad is doing in there?" I got out of the car to see if I could spot him. I walked a few yards toward the door of the gas station. I saw him at the end of a line and came back to the car.

"People must be buying lottery tickets," I told Noah. Within a few minutes, Mike finally came out.

"That took you forever. What was going on?" I said.

"The clerk was having trouble with someone's credit card."

We both went around to the hatch of the car and poured the ice over the beer. "We'll probably need more ice tomorrow. It's pretty hot tonight."

We drove off toward the hotel. It was dark and past Noah's bedtime.

"My pants are down," Noah said.

"What?" we both said.

"My pants are down," he said again from the back seat, more loudly.

"Your pants can't be down. We'll be at the hotel in a minute," I said. I twisted around to look into the dark backseat but couldn't see anything as Noah was directly behind me.

"My pants are down."

"Okay. We're here." Mike pulled into the hotel parking lot.

We opened Noah's car door and yes, his pants were down. Around his ankles were his elastic waist shorts and his underwear. He was sitting in the plastic car seat sans pants.

"Wow. Your pants *are* down and your underpants, too," I said.

"He's naked in the car seat," Mike said. "How the hell did that happen? Did you buckle him in without his pants up?"

"Well, no. No way. I would have noticed something as obvious as his pants being down, don't you think?"

"I'd think so. What about when you got out of the car at the gas station?"

"I didn't really leave the car for more than a few seconds, just to walk up to see where you were. There wasn't anyone around. No one that I noticed anyway," I said.

"Noah? Did someone pull your pants down at the gas station?" Mike asked.

"No," he said.

"Are you sure that no one came up to the car while Mom wasn't looking?"

"No!" he said.

"He couldn't have undone the straps, that's for sure," said Mike. At three, Noah's cerebral palsy had already given him hand weakness and coordination troubles. He could hardly feed himself and he'd never taken his own pants up or down even in the best of circumstances—much less in a car seat.

"Well how the hell did his pants get down?" Mike said.

"Do you suppose… I mean this is really strange. But do you think the spirit of Houdini did it?" I said, speculating. I really didn't believe in ghosts but had no other explanation.

"Maybe he was mad that we didn't make it to the museum. Maybe this was his way of letting us know we should have tried harder. It would have taken someone like Houdini to get those pants off without undoing the car seat and without us knowing," said Mike.

"Noah, do you think Houdini made your pants go down?" one of us asked.

"Maybe…" he said.

The story is family legend now, and when Mike and I tell the story about the de-pantsing of Noah in Appleton, we have no more concrete evidence about it now than we did in 1991. We know it happened and we can't explain it—over the years we'd ask Noah about it. He'd smile a sly smile and offer no more information than we already had.

Maybe like Houdini, Noah needed some escape from the restraints that held him. The ankle-foot orthotics, the braces and devices he had to wear on his body each day were his chains. "Ahh," he'd sigh as I un-Velcroed his feet or wrists at the end of the day. No matter how carefully molded, created and padded, the plastic devices always left a mark. I'd gently rub the pink-reddish indents on his soft white skin until the color returned to normal and the dent disappeared. But each day the ankle-foot orthotics and braces were back on his body, straightening and fixing what wasn't working. I don't think Noah was ever trying to escape us, or his life, though I wonder sometimes why escaping came to him so often. Whether he was escaping his pants or chuckling about Wilbur the pig's run from the pen, or backing away from a complicated story, the fast break was something he liked. For Mike and I, Noah's inexplicable escape from his pants while buckled in his car seat was just one more thing that made life with our son magical.

chapter 5 | Bluffton School

School Days.

One summer evening we officially enrolled Noah at Bluffton School during a "Kindergarten Roundup" event. I loved the image of trying to round up five-year-old kids—all full of energy and curiosity—moving around, touching everything and talking all the time. The shy ones hiding behind their parents needed rounding up, too. Noah was the only kid in a wheelchair at the roundup and the kids were curious about it. They spoke softly and pointed.

"Why can't he walk?"

"Is he hurt?"

"What is that thing?"

"Why is he in a wheelchair?"

"Why are his legs so skinny?"

I did my best to answer them. I didn't get into the specifics of his cerebral palsy but gave them what I thought were kid-logical answers. I didn't want to embarrass him. Noah seemed a little sheepish, looking away or up at me, sometimes biting his lip. He nodded along as I tried to explain. These were questions that we'd come to answer throughout Noah's life, though I'd not anticipated them this evening. I faked my way around things, trying to make his disability seem normal and not so scary.

"His legs just don't work really well. He can stand a little, but walking is much harder."

"Maybe one day he'll be able to walk, but until then he uses the chair."

"No, he's not hurt. He was just born this way."

"He's in a wheelchair because he can't walk and we have places to go."

"It's called a wheelchair. It helps him get from place to place, like your legs or your bike help you."

"His legs are skinny because he doesn't walk, so they have a hard time getting big and strong like yours," I said as I patted Noah's bony knee.

The kids were fresh-faced and cute, and all I wanted was for them to like and accept Noah.

A bright blue-eyed, freckle-faced tomboy worked her way to the front of the group.

"Can I push him?" she asked.

"You'll have to ask Noah," I said. "What's your name?"

"I'm Jordan," she said. "Does he know how to talk?" she asked me.

I nodded. Noah hadn't said much while the kids were quizzing me.

"Noah, can I push your chair?" she asked.

"Okay," Noah said, and the two of them were off and down the hall from the gym where we were all gathered. Jordan could barely see over the back of the chair. They careened back and forth down the well-polished hall, lined with coat hooks, shelves and cubbies. It smelled of wax and lemon-scented cleaner, soon to be replaced with kid-scented boots, coats, forgotten lunchboxes and spilled milk. The late summer sun beamed into the hall from the classrooms where doors were open. It was bright, and I couldn't see them as they traveled.

Other kids lined up for the chance to push the chair.

"Let me! Let me push him."

"It's my turn now."

Noah couldn't stop smiling.

I didn't have a plan or any solid ideas about how to integrate Noah into the kindergarten class but that appeared to be taking care of itself, for now.

As the kids were joyriding with Noah, I filled out the papers and went to the registration table.

"It looks as if Noah will need a healthcare aide," said the principal, looking over the shoulder of the secretary.

"Oh. What does that mean?" I wasn't sure about the word healthcare. I knew Noah needed help doing things in school, but healthcare seemed like an odd word for a school to use.

"He or she would help Noah with getting to the bathroom, eating lunch and participating in classroom activities and lessons," he said.

"In the PPI class at McLaughlin School, Noah had some services that I'd like him to have here, too," I said.

"What might those be?" he said, in a slightly unreceptive voice.

People at Noah's Special Ed preschool had warned me that Bluffton School wasn't used to special needs students and had encouraged me to send him to a bigger school with more disabled kids. I resisted. I wanted him to get to know the kids who lived nearby, and Bluffton was a sweet place. Nestled between two sand dunes, protected from the winds of Lake Michigan, the small school had a reputation for its close community, parental involvement and high academic achievement. I still believed that one day Noah could, no would, walk and live like an able-bodied kid, and he needed to have friends who were his equal. Bluffton was a good place to forge those ties.

"He needs speech, physical and occupational therapies," I said with confidence. The secretary took notes without looking up. "And the healthcare aide," I said. I knew that Michigan law and the American with Disabilities Act would provide the resources to help him be part of the classroom and receive instruction like the other kids.

"Are there other accommodations he'll need?" the principal asked.

"Maybe a toilet chair in the bathroom?" I asked, testing to see what school personnel might say. I'd learned that durable medical equipment was expensive and getting it into schools or even our own home was an ordeal. But, when Noah started school a few weeks later, his classroom was stocked with the equipment I'd requested so he could be integrated into Bluffton School.

After filling out the papers and watching Noah fly through the hall, we all gathered in the spacious classroom. Its big windows opened onto sand dunes, grasses, scrub trees, oaks, pines, black squirrels and the occasional deer. Mr. Johnson, the teacher, introduced himself. It was his first year of teaching; he was young, earnest and eager to meet the kids. Mr. Johnson was tall, about six feet six inches, which made most kindergarteners about thigh high when they stood near him. In the kindergarten room that night, he sat on a kid's chair and his new students, his first real class, sat in a circle around him. Mr. Johnson was all legs and feet as he leaned low making eye contact with the cross-legged kids around him. I took Noah out of his chair and sat on the edge of the circle with him leaning against me, since he couldn't sit up on his own. Mr. Johnson asked the kids to go around the circle and say their names. Moms and dads coached the shy and reluctant.

"You can see we have centers all around the room. Each day we'll work in the centers on skill building—learning and writing our letters, colors, shapes, math skills and reading," he said. He told the kids about the school rules and his expectations for them as good citizens. He asked the kids if they had any questions.

"When is recess?"

"Where is the bathroom?"

"I'm scared."

"Can I bring my dog to school?"

Noah liked his new teacher. All the other kids called him Mr. Johnson, but Noah couldn't get out the Mister so he just called him Johnson. Noah's speech was delayed and now in kindergarten he was just starting to use simple sentences and to understand he had a voice. If he needed something during class, he'd call out, "Johnson! Help me," and Johnson would come to his assistance.

Johnson took extra time with Noah, and he helped Noah's healthcare aide, Kitty, figure out how to deliver the lessons and practices. Noah was a great listener and could remember most information that was read to him. He took all of his tests through school with someone reading the questions to him. He was an auditory learner, which was great because Kitty was a talker.

She called herself *Pretty Kitty* and was one of twelve siblings from a large Irish Catholic family in Muskegon. Kitty was short, round, with happy blue eyes and reddish brown hair. One of her brothers had Down syndrome, so she was comfortable and capable with people with disabilities. She started as Noah's healthcare aide in kindergarten and stayed with him until middle school. Kitty worked hard to help him understand and participate in the classroom lessons and activities. She ran his wheelchair around the gym. "Noah, you're going to kill me with this class," she said. From stretching his tight hands and heel cords and practicing speech therapy lessons with him, she served as a physical/occupational therapy aide.

Kitty helped him eat snacks; she laid him down on the kindergarten rug for rest and took him out for recess, helping him bounce a ball or turn a jump rope. She hoisted him onto swings and toilets and was the second set of hands that helped him write his ABCs and work the scissors that cut out shapes. It is her handwriting over his that created school Mother's and Father's Day cards and holiday decorations.

Kitty was incredibly patient and she was inventive, finding new ways to help Noah do his schoolwork. She talked to him continually, and her engaging sense of humor came across as he formed his own ideas of what was funny. He'd come home from school with the punch line of a joke or riddle that Kitty taught him, and we'd have to try to decipher what the joke might be. Over time he absorbed her sense of humor and language nuances, so we were thankful to have an aide whose personality we enjoyed.

I kept a notebook in Noah's backpack. In it, Kitty and I would write about what was going on at school and home. Noah wasn't one to tell either of us anything. I looked forward to reading her notes from school each evening and writing to her in the morning.

Me: *Noah slept badly last night. He's crabby this morning. Watch out.*

Kitty: *Noah would not do his work this morning. Johnson had a talk with him and he shaped up. When Orrie took blocks away from Noah, he pinched him. Noah said he was sorry and cried when we talked with him about it.*

Me: *We spoke sharply to Noah about pinching. He said he was sorry, but then he pinched my neck and laughed. He used to be so sweet. I think you are ruining him, Kitty. Grandpa Bob will pick him up at school today. They're going to lunch somewhere.*

Kitty: *Tomorrow is the 100th day of school. Everyone in the class needs to bring in one hundred of something to count. Please send me a hundred ten dollar bills.*

Me: *Sorry, I was short on $10s. Noah's stuff is in his backpack. Have fun counting today.*

Kitty: *Really? Wine bottle corks. The other kids brought in pennies, candy, stones, crayons and Noah has wine bottle corks. We're calling protective services.*

Me: *It was Noah's idea.*

For seven years we wrote back and forth. Some accounts were short, others longer, but the minutiae of his school days was detailed between Kitty and me.

During that first year of school, Noah teamed up with three girls—Regina, Abby and Megan. The girls became best friends and included Noah in some of their activities. He went to their birthday parties and they came to his. They were good chair pushers and helped him with his mittens and hat in winter. Regina's mom ran a daycare business and Noah went there after school, which solidified their friendship. It's hard to find in-home daycare providers to take a kid in a wheelchair, but Cindy had a big heart and an accessible home. It was she who ensured Noah was included in the girl's events and activities. Regina was tender and helped him with his snacks. They played games and she read to him. She was probably his best friend throughout his life.

Noah's first big crush was on Abby, though. At five years old, she was a head taller than the rest of the kids, slender with shiny, straight brown hair cut in a bob. She was not shy, but quiet and artistically introspective. Her tacked up drawings and coloring pages stood out among the rest of the kindergarten student art.

By land, Abby lived a couple of miles from us, but by boat she was just a few minutes away. We'd launch our aluminum fishing boating from the dock near our house, with Noah in a big floatable seat strapped to the boat bench, and we'd putter around in Muskegon Lake and Lake Michigan. In warm months, I'd make a picnic and we would head out, anchor or drift, eat supper and enjoy being on the water.

"So, Noah, where do you want to go today—big lake or little lake?"

"By Abby's house," he always said.

We'd launch and head south on Muskegon Lake toward her house. As we drew closer, Mike would slow the boat down and we'd hug the shore.

"Abby. Abby," Noah would say, looking toward her house. Noah would shout her name, hoping to get her attention, but really he couldn't be heard over the buzz of the outboard motor. Sometimes we'd see her through the picture window at the dining room table that overlooked the water. She might be eating dinner with her family or doing what appeared to be making art at the table. Usually, we'd turn back and make a couple of passes to attract her eye. She'd eventually look up and come to the window and wave at Noah.

"Abby's waving," he'd say. "Abby … " his face was blissful.

Noah stayed at Bluffton until the fourth grade, when it became clear he needed additional Special Education services, and segregation rather than integration would be best for his long-term learning. His academic ability was dropping below the rest of his class, and it wasn't possible for him to keep up anymore. We were starting to accept that his intellectual abilities weren't on par with his classmates despite the immersion. We'd given him the very best integrated public education we could, but he needed more. We moved him to a different school; it was bigger, with long interconnected halls, a maze to navigate. It was hard to say goodbye to innocent and gentle Bluffton School, perfect for first friendships and early learning. Each spring we returned there for the school carnival where everyone remembered him. The kids and teachers greeted Noah with genuine warmth. He would smile, talk with his teachers and old classmates, laugh and play the goofy games, all the while keeping an eye out for Kitty, Johnson and, of course, Abby.

chapter 6 | Swedish Christmas

Star Boy.

Maybe the old Swedes were surprised the first time they saw a Yulebumpkin in a wheelchair. But after six years in the program, Noah had advanced to full-blown Star Boy, and people at the club were used to seeing him in the St. Lucia Day celebration.

When I was thirteen years old, I was St. Lucia at the Viking Lodge, a Scandinavian social club, in Muskegon. Like Lucia before me, I wore a long white gown with a bright red sash around the waist, and a crown of candles (battery-powered to avoid flaming hair) sat upon my head. The privilege of representing Lucia was given to the oldest Junior Viking girl who had *done time* in the program. I'd been in the court for Wendy and Sonja before taking over the duties of St. Lucia, who led the procession of boys, girls and toddlers who were Yulebumpkins (little elves), Tomtens (older, mischievous elves) and Star Boys (older boys and sometimes girls, if there is a boy shortage). Fully costumed and well-rehearsed, the extravaganza takes place each year around December 13.

I was delighted when Mrs. Matthews, the club's St. Lucia organizer, first called and invited Noah to be in the program. She was calling down a list of the junior member's parents, recruiting kids for the show. "Would Noah like to be in the St. Lucia pageant this year?" she asked.

"Yes, yes. Of course," I replied. Noah was five at the time and had been recently fitted for his first little wheelchair. "But he can't propel himself. He'll need a helper to push him."

Mrs. Matthews paused for a moment and mumbled, checking a list of names. I began to worry. "I think we can find someone to help. Maybe one of the Star Boys," she said. I was surprised, really.

I expected that Noah would be excluded from the program. Not that Scandinavian people have an issue with disability, but this is a program steeped in tradition and routine, and a wheelchair had never been part of it before now.

At rehearsal, Noah was given a little pair of red footie pajamas and a Santa cap with an elastic chin strap. He pulled on the elastic and snapped himself.

"Ow. Ow. This hat hurts," he said. "Tight, it's tight."

"You only have to wear it for a little bit. Don't mess with it, and you'll be okay," I said.

Mrs. Matthews assigned a Star Boy to push Noah's wheelchair. She was an elementary school teacher and was seasoned at directing kids. I could tell that the chosen boy was clearly not into this. Pushing a kid in a wheelchair in a goofy Christmas program wasn't cool. I could see his eyes rolling.

"You and Noah can lead the Yulebumpkin group. Just follow the last Tomtem," she said to the Star Boy pusher. There were six little kids similarly dressed as Noah at the end of the twenty-kid procession. Lucia led, followed by her entourage of Lucia girls, then Star Boys, Tomten, and finally the Yulebumpkins. The two-through-four-year-old Yulebumpkins were whacking each other with dinner plate-size stars on sticks, falling out of line, stopping to gawk at the audience, running into one another as they gaped, crying, and sometimes running off to the arms of a parent. One became a diva and stole the spotlight with a personal dance and star waving performance.

"Noah, just hold your star up nice and high and remember to smile," I coached him before they began. He lowered his star on a stick and frowned at me.

"Come on Noah," I said. "Grandma is going to want to get pictures. You need to keep your star up." The star remained at half-mast.

"Hey," I said to the attendant Star Boy, "Remind him to hold his star up. And be careful not to run the Tomtens over. The front of the wheelchair sticks out kind of far," I said. The Star Boy gave me a blank look.

The Viking member choir, accompanied by two accordions and a flute, sang the Italian-revised-by-Swedes carol "Santa Lucia" as the children slowly proceeded around the lodge. Built in the 1970s, the lodge was vast and echoey with a slippery wooden dance floor in its center. The focal point was a bar, a wood replica of a Viking ship complete with a dragon's head. Bartenders stood down inside the "ship" and served up strong, cheap drinks to members—people who were of Scandinavian descent or claimed to be.

The Swedes and parents and grandparents of kids got misty and sipped glogg as the choir sang the old familiar song. The entire procession took several minutes to make the circuit of the lodge. Noah's star was near his feet and he was looking around for us. As he wheeled by our table I whispered, "Get your star up." He waved it up fast, and then it was down again.

Mrs. Matthews told the story of St. Lucia and Christmas in Sweden which went something like this:

"December 13 is the feast day of St. Lucia—she's the patron saint of the blind and is known for bringing light to the world. St. Lucia was a woman who vowed her life to the service of Christ and declined to marry a pagan man and then gave her dowry to the poor people of Syracuse, Sicily. Her pagan fiancée denounced her faith to authorities and she was to be burned at the stake. When she did not go up in smoke, the guards took her eyes out with a fork. In some tellings of the story, the evil fiancée took her eyes because they were so pretty. Swedes adopted her as their own icon and in the 1900s began having the Lucia Day (Lucia Daagen) Celebration on December 13, which by the pre-Gregorian calendar was the longest, darkest day of the year or the winter solstice. It is the first day of the Christmas season in Sweden, which carries through to Epiphany, St. Knut's Day and almost into Lent."

As Mrs. Matthews told the beloved story, Lucia stood front and center, her crown of candles all aglow, and Noah waved his star on a stick all around.

We returned to be in the program the following year and the year after that. Noah advanced to Tomten—he wore red pants, a grey shirt and a red cap with a giant poofy tassel. He carried a lantern and let it rest between his feet on the footrest of the wheelchair. Another Christmas passed and he was promoted to Star Boy, wearing a white gown, which looked like a choir robe cut in half. He wore a cone-shaped hat painted with gold glitter stars.

"Noah is a cone head," Mike teased. "He looks like he's in the KKK." I threw him a dirty look. "You have no appreciation of my Swedish culture," I said.

As a Star Boy, Noah was issued a star on a stick just like he was when he was a little kid, but unlike when he was younger he held the star up the whole time, totally blocking the face of one of the Lucia girls who was too polite to tell him to move it. Over time, things have changed with his Star Boy pusher, too. The boys became used to Noah. Instead of being freaked out by a kid in a chair, when they saw him each year, they jockeyed to push.

"I'll push Noah," said one of the kids.

"Nah. Noah and I go to school together. I'll push him."

"Let me. I did it last year. I know how."

It wasn't that they were friends with Noah or anything. I wouldn't fool myself with that idea. But it appeared to be cooler to push Star Boy in a wheelchair than to walk around carrying a star on a stick.

chapter 7 | Nervous

With the Woodland Mall Santa.

Noah loved Christmas, and we fueled his passion with our own holiday hype. We're super hall-deckers. There's not a surface in our house that doesn't have some piece of Christmas crud on it. Elves on shelves. A manger with a major menagerie. In the bathroom a rooftop Kleenex box topper with a pulled tissue that looks like chimney smoke. A bobble head Santa. Angels in high and low places. A super-groovy Christmas red wax lava lamp. We set up miniature figurines of the entire cast of Rudolph the Red Nosed Reindeer accompanied by a large, animated Bumble with stiff white fur. Central to our celebration is a big, fake tree. It is lit like Tokyo-at-night-fully-ornamented, set-up-the-day-after-Thanksgiving-until-Epiphany-or-St. Knut's Day. At our house, Christmas was never a day, but a season.

Shortly after his late September birthday, Noah began his Christmas quizzing.

"How many more days to Christmas?"

"How do reindeer fly?"

"How many elves are there?" And the random, "Does Santa really love me?"

For years we played along. Mike and I liked the innocence and the imagination that surrounded Noah during the holidays. Even when he was in the third grade and someone told him (again) that there was no Santa, we acted shocked.

"What? Who said that? They are in such trouble. If you don't believe, you won't receive," I said. "Santa-denying is a very bad thing."

"Really?" said Noah.

"If you want to believe in Santa, that's okay. Dad and I do, and you can too. You don't have to go along with the kids at school. Believe what you want to believe." Noah was a little naïve, a little too trusting of Mike and me. He relied on us, not only for his mobility and day-to-day care, but also for much of his life information outside the classroom. Sometimes the worldview we provided was laced with imagination, irony and truth-stretching. We didn't see any good reason to be truthful on this point. The realities of life are harsh, and believing in someone like Santa was harmless enough and fun for all of us.

Noah did seem suspicious of other kids' anti-Santa claims, but was hesitant to question us too strongly on our defense, on the chance of jeopardizing his relationship with the great gift-bearer.

"When can I go see Santa?" he asked me around Halloween.

"That's going to be awhile," I said. "You have all of November and some of December to wait. You don't want to go too early because Santa could forget. You don't want to go too late because he might be out of things. We have to time it *just* right."

"When's that?" he said.

"Around December 10."

Noah held me to that date, checking the days on the calendar after Thanksgiving. We'd see Santa out and about while shopping, and Noah would crane his neck as we wheeled by.

"Now? Can't we go now?" he said, hopeful that I'd let him slide in early.

"No. Not yet. Still too early."

"Those kids are with Santa Claus."

"Yes, they are. You'll get your chance," I said. "Do you have your list ready?"

"Not really."

"Well, then. There you go. No need to see Santa today. Let's get that list in shape," I said.

We didn't make a paper list. We just talked about the things Noah wanted and needed, and his job was to remember the list when he finally got to see Santa. "It's more sincere that way," I told him.

"Buzz Lightyear. Talking Woody. Race cars. Charlie Brown DVDs," he recited, working on his memorizing.

"All good stuff. How about some pajamas? A new jacket? How about some underwear? You can always use underwear," I teased.

"No underwear," he said. "I'm not asking Santa for *that*."

The Saturday we all headed to visit Santa was cold and clear, unusual for West Michigan which tends to be gloomy in the winter. The sun was out, and there was a thin layer of new snow on the ground. Mike and I bundled Noah in a jacket and mittens and loaded him and his wheelchair into the back of the van.

"Are you ready to talk with Santa?" I asked.

"I'm nervous," Noah said.

"Why are you nervous? You've seen Santa plenty of times before. It'll be fine. Just remember your list. And be polite," I said.

"I'm nervous."

He looked nervous; his face was flushed and slightly sweaty. Perhaps I'd put too much pressure on him with memorizing the list and all.

"Dad and I will be there with you. There's nothing to be concerned about," I said.

As we stood near the mall's North Pole chalet, an authentic-looking Santa motioned toward us with a white-gloved hand. We looked around, up and down the line, not quite knowing for sure who was getting the wave. Santa sent a helper to fetch Noah.

"Come on up here," she said. "Santa says he's been waiting to see you."

Noah's eyes widened, and he sat up tall in his wheelchair. His involuntary startle reflexes took over and his feet kicked the footplate of his chair and his hand flung out to the side. Noah possessed an over-developed startle reflex from his cerebral palsy. Basketball game buzzers, an automatic flush toilet in an airport restroom, a surprise scene in a movie, or any loud voice, bang, boom or pop would send him into a spasm.

"It's okay, Noah," I said. I looked at the helper. "He can't help the flailing."

She smiled, and we pushed on up to Santa, who came down from his Santa chair and knelt close to Noah, putting his arm around the back of the wheelchair.

"What's your name?"

"Noah," our son whispered. Santa's hearing must have been excellent.

"Well, Noah," he said in a normal, not too ho-ho or loud voice. "Have you been good this year?"

"Yes," Noah squeaked.

"I thought so. What would you like for Christmas this year?"

Noah paused. His eyes gazed heavenward as he worked to recall his list. He pulled in his bottom lip. His hand clenched and relaxed. A long stretch of seconds passed. It felt like hours to Mike and me.

"Well?" Santa said kindly.

Then, in voice loud enough for people nearby to hear he blurted, "Underwear. I want underwear!"

Santa looked surprised. Mike and I laughed. Noah blushed and looked at his feet.

"Is that all?"

"Yes," Noah said.

"That's a good thing to want for Christmas," Santa said. He was trying not to laugh. "I'm sure my elves can find some other presents for you, too," he said.

Noah sighed. "Thanks."

We thanked Santa, too.

"Wait, we need a picture of this young man with me," he said. He wheeled Noah over near the painted backdrop of pine trees, a glowing cabin and snow.

"On the count of three, smile," said the photographer.

Noah smiled, knowing, believing that Santa would take care of him.

| Pumpkin Indecision

Where the pumpkin obsession began.

We drove the van down Apple Avenue in mid-October, heading east toward Ravenna, a small rural town ten miles to the east. I hoped we wouldn't have to go that far for a pumpkin. Noah was in the front seat of the van. Usually he rode in his wheelchair, strapped in by the second row of seats, but on days like this when we were in no hurry, I'd lift him up into the front seat so we could chat and listen to music.

He was probably twelve years old, still pretty small and light for his age, so lifting him into the seat was easy. He crossed his legs at the knee, one foot on the floor and the other one swinging casually.

"How about some Jimmy Buffett?" he said. He liked the familiar songs and would sing along a few words now and again.

It was a half-day of school. Mike and I switched off these days at home with Noah, and I lucked out with this one. It was warm for October and the day was sunny with big clouds in the bright blue sky. The farms we passed were ringed with maple and oak trees. The burgundy, red, yellow and orange leaves were paint box pretty. We rode along pointing out stands of trees we liked, oohing and ahhing like we did for fireworks. We slowed for various pumpkin wagons and patches.

"How about this one?" I said, slowing the van and powering the window down so Noah could look at the choices. Because we had to control so much of what went on with him in his day-to-day life, it was fun to play along that choosing the best pumpkin was important. He thought it was funny, too.

"No. Not here," Noah said.

"Not sincere enough?"

Noah laughed. "Not sincere at all."

The quest for a sincere pumpkin patch stemmed from watching *It's the Great Pumpkin Charlie Brown* on video each Halloween. Noah latched onto the idea of a sincere pumpkin patch, and would settle for nothing less. We never bought pumpkins at the grocery store, gas station or even the farmer's market. We always found them at a farm or roadside stand. When Noah was three, we took him to a pumpkin patch and cider mill between Fremont and White Cloud, towns to our northeast. He had a crown of blonde fluffy curls framing his head and he wore a little jean jacket that day. I took a photo of him, kneeling behind a huge pumpkin, surrounded by hundreds of other smaller ones. It was the photo that we used for a Christmas card that year. Perhaps it was that very early experience that set his destiny for choosing a pumpkin each year. He was very particular about his pumpkins.

We drove a bit longer and a wooden sign with "Pumpkins" painted on it directed us to turn left onto Broton Road. About a mile down the road, just when I started to question if I had actually seen the sign, there was a farmhouse, a red barn and four flatbed wagons full of pumpkins.

"This looks good, Mom."

"Okay. This is it, then. Let's find some pumpkins."

I went to the back of the van, took Noah's wheelchair down the lift and placed him in it.

Rolling him over the hard packed dirt and grass, bouncing along over ruts and ridges, we stopped at the first wagon.

"These are the little ones," Noah said.

"Looks like they get bigger as we go along. Do you want a little one or a bigger one?"

"We need three. Mine, yours and Dad's."

"Oh. Okay. We're all getting pumpkins, are we?" I asked.

Noah nodded, "Mmmhmm."

"I think I'll take one of these little ones. Here, hold it for me." I plopped the pumpkin in his lap so I could push his wheelchair. He gripped it with both hands. It reminded me a little of the first pumpkin patch experience from years ago.

We moved down to the middle sizes and to the center of the wagon so Noah could get a good view of his choices. I pointed out some interesting vegetables. Tall, skinny ones. Short, fat ones. Pumpkins with warts and pumpkins with flat sides perfect for carving. Light orange ones, and some with big curly stems. Pumpkin after pumpkin didn't pass the only-in-his-head secret perfect pumpkin test.

We wheeled around the wagon hoping the other side had better choices. Noah pointed out a possibility. I brought it down to his eye level and he shook his head no. We meandered a bit further. I offered more options.

"Nope," he said. I took a deep breath. His charming indecision was becoming annoying. His control of the situation started to wear thin.

"Noah, pick one for your Dad. You can keep looking for yours." I picked out two good-looking specimens—put them on the edge of the wagon. "Choose one for Dad. Now."

"I think he would like that one," Noah said, choosing a tall pumpkin. I set it down near the wheel of the wagon.

"How ya doin'?" said the pumpkin proprietor walking toward us. He wore jeans and a faded green t-shirt with a pocket on the chest. His summer tan was starting to fade, but the creases around his eyes and mouth were still white lines.

"Looking for something special?"

"Just looking for one more perfect pumpkin," I said.

"Let me know if you need some help. We got lots of them. Big ones down there, little ones over here. Got some cornstalks and gourds if you need that," he said trying to be helpful.

"Thanks," Noah and I said at the same time as we wheeled over to the large pumpkin wagon.

The farmer followed along, whistling softly. The tune was familiar, but I couldn't quite place it. His whistling was remarkable, really. I imagined he sang in the church choir, too. I thought of requesting a song, just to test him.

"Here's some nice ones," he said pointing out some huge pumpkins. Noah smiled. "Those are really big," I said of the championship-sized vegetables.

"I can get it into your van, if you need help."

"Thanks, but I can handle a pumpkin, I lift *him* all the time," I said nodding toward Noah.

"He doesn't look like he weighs much more than a pumpkin himself," he said with a grin.

"Noah, do you want a big one?"

"No, I don't think so."

We wheeled back to the small pumpkin wagon. I took the tall pumpkin under my arm and did my best to push the chair with one hand. I turned the chair around and bumped Noah backwards over the ground. I knew Noah was doing his best to control and orchestrate this situation. And I was doing my best to be patient and let him.

At the small pumpkin wagon I showed Noah some more options. "This?" I asked.

He shook his head no.

"I like this one."

"Which one?" I asked. He clutched my small pumpkin as he didn't have a hand to point.

"This one," he said nodding downward.

"My pumpkin? You want *my* pumpkin?" I said, feigning shock.

"It's mine now."

I laughed. "Yes, it seems to fit you well. I guess I need to find my pumpkin now."

The farmer came around and offered to take the pumpkin I was holding under my arm. I handed it to him.

"We just need one more," I said.

"Come on, Mom, just pick one," Noah said loudly.

I wanted to tell the farmer it wasn't me that was the hold up and that my son had commandeered my pumpkin, but he looked like he had real work to do. I grabbed another small pumpkin, put it in Noah's lap with the other, and handed the farmer ten dollars as he walked us to the van.

We drove away, heading west with the late autumn sun almost in our eyes. I pulled down the visor on his side so he wouldn't need to squint. Noah held the small pumpkin in his lap and looked out at the trees. He seemed quite pleased with himself; he got what he wanted, not only in the pumpkins, but in his ability to make me do what he wanted for a change.

CHAPTER 9 | Riding Red Man

Old pony.

Before the horseback-riding lesson began, Noah and I wheeled around the barn bumping over uneven concrete floors, peeking at horses in the stalls.

"Maybe you'll ride this one," I said, as I helped Noah stand on the footrests of his wheelchair to see the horse. He grabbed the stall door and pulled himself up, his chin resting on the rough top board. Standing in the pen was a sweet looking brown horse. According to the paper tacked on a post, his name was CQ.

"Hi, CQ," I said. The horse lifted his head and looked at us. Unlike some of the other horses that had warning signs posted near their stalls with messages like "I Bite" or "Don't Feed Me" there were no warnings for CQ.

Noah reached out and petted his muzzle. And as horses often do, he sneezed, with a loud, juicy explosion. Noah's hand flew off CQ's nose and he nearly leapt from his wheelchair and over the gate. The equally surprised equine stepped back.

"Whoa, Noah!" I said and I helped him settle back into his chair. "Horses make some pretty funny noises."

"When can I ride?" he said.

"It's almost time. Let's look at the other horses." We wheeled on.

"Phew. It smells like poop," said Noah, laughing. At the age of ten, he found poop, farting, boogers and bad smells of any sort to be a source of amusement.

"Horses poop a lot. Big old piles of poop," I said. He giggled and then wiggled. Noah's full body wiggle was another involuntary response. The wiggle came on when he was happy about something or if he thought something was funny or when he was in trouble. It was a nervous reaction; he couldn't control it any more than he could control the startle reflex.

"Everyone poops," he said, referring to the title of a book he liked.

"Yes, everyone poops, but horses, they poop even more than you do. I hope you don't roll through any horse poop with your chair," I said, knowing this would make him wiggle, which it did.

Noah's physical therapist, Colleen, suggested we try the riding program. She thought it would help improve his balance and trunk strength. Noah was keen on the idea. Trips to 4-H fairs and reading books like *Misty of Chincoteague* piqued his interest in horses. Mike and I were eager to do anything that might give Noah a new experience and help him physically. The lessons began in mid-April at West Michigan Therapeutic Horsemanship, located on a rutted dirt road east of here near Coopersville. This was not a fancy riding program like the one in suburban Grand Rapids. The horse barn was drafty with bales of straw for seats in the helmet room, rustic stalls with hook and eye latches, and the tack and saddles hung from nails on the walls. A haze of dust and a freckling of flies filled the air. Not dirty or run-down—just horsey and basic.

People were beginning to gather at the end of the barn: a boy with a walker, a young girl in a wheelchair, an older boy with a cognitive impairment and several teen volunteers. We joined them. The leader of the program was a wholesome woman named Jeri. She was tough-voiced, but very gentle with her special needs students. She welcomed us and gave the students instructions. "You'll need to brush the horses before riding. We'll help saddle them up for you. They need brushing after riding, too," she said. She told us we would be walking in the ring, practicing steering and playing games. Brushing the horse was part of the learning experience; through it, Noah would gain hand strength, coordination and form a bond with his horse. It was also his chance to care for something, instead of being taken care of.

"Go ahead now. Take a brush and a currycomb. If you haven't brushed a horse before, a volunteer will show you how," Jeri said. I took one of each brush, and set them in Noah's lap. We wheeled out into corral through the soft, dirty sand that is common in West Michigan. Pushing wasn't easy and the small front tires of the wheelchair got stuck. I pulled the chair onto its back two wheels, turned it around and pulled Noah toward Jeri.

"Noah, you'll be riding Red Man," she said motioning toward a horse tied to a fence. Red Man was the most bedraggled beast I'd ever seen. He was skinny, his back swayed and his hipbones stuck out. He was short, about waist high to me. True to his name, he was a reddish color and very shaggy. His nose sprouted hundreds of white old man whiskers. He looked like he had one hoof in the grave and the other in the dog food factory. He was a wreck of a horse.

"Noah, that horse is as skinny as you are."

"I like him," Noah said.

We wheeled over to Red Man, and a teenage girl came over to help with the brushing. Noah wiggled. He wiggled, too, when he saw a pretty girl. We knew at an early age that playing poker would never be for him—his wiggle was his emotional barometer and gave away his feelings.

The perky blonde volunteer put her hand over Noah's with the currycomb, and showed him how to brush the little beast. Hair flew everywhere. I was astounded at the amount of dander, dust and hair coming off Red Man, much of it settling onto Noah's lap.

"These horses always are pretty hairy at the start of the season. They're losing their winter coats," she said.

"Dirty," Noah said.

"More like dusty," I said. "You're the one who wanted to ride horses, so let's get him cleaned up." Noah continued making circular motions with the currycomb. Despite ten minutes of brushing, Red Man still looked scruffy. Noah switched sides and began working on the horse's flank. I took a soft brush and tried to make the best of the opposite side. Red Man liked it and began leaning toward Noah. The old horse leaned so hard that I wondered if he would end up in Noah's lap. I eased up on the brush, but Red Man continued to lean. "He's on me!" Noah said. The volunteer gave Red Man a shove back toward me to upright him. She held a saddle in her arms, which she put over the fence. Red Man sniffed the saddle with suspicion.

"Noah, you need to go into the barn and choose a blanket and some reins," the volunteer said.

Back into the barn we went, returning the grooming implements to a barrel. We chose some pretty blue reins and a thick brown blanket. I threw them on Noah's lap and we went back out to the ring. The volunteer showed Noah how to clip the reins and put the blanket on the horse. She did the saddling, and Jeri came around and approved the job.

"Red Man's a good old horse," she said.

"How old is he?" I asked.

"He's around thirty this year. Red Man is about to retire. He's been at this quite a few years, and he's getting kind of pokey," she said, rubbing him behind his ear.

"Pokey is good. Noah's never ridden a horse before."

"Well, Noah, are you ready?" asked Jeri.

"Ready!" he said, smiling like he'd won a prize.

Since Noah was new to the program, Fred, Jeri's husband, was recruited to help him ride. He and I lifted Noah onto Red Man, who started to step side to side. Luckily, his reins were tied to the fence. Fred spoke sternly to Red Man; the horse continued to dodge Noah, who was alternating between wiggling and stiffening up. "Relax, Noah," I said, useless words because Noah can't relax on command. Fred grabbed Noah's leg and worked his foot into the stirrup while I tried to balance Noah on the horse. Fred held Noah, and I shoved the other foot into the stirrup. Adjustments were made on the reins and shorter stirrups were needed; the riding helmet slipped over Noah's eyes. There was so much going on. The horse moved, Noah wobbled. Dust floated and flies flew. I wondered what kind of therapy would be had.

For some reason, I'd envisioned Noah would sit on the horse and ride unencumbered, or that there would be a special needs saddle to support him. The "device" was Fred on one side and me on the other. Both of us supported Noah on the horse—one hand on his back, another on his leg or chest. Noah holds the reins with an iron grip; at least the clenched fists from his cerebral palsy were useful in this activity.

His job was to steer the horse, though it was clear Red Man had been around the ring a few times and didn't need much directing. Noah grinned as he took his first ride around the corral. It wasn't easy keeping him astride the horse—a moment without a hand in the right place and Noah listed off to one side or another. My nose itched from the dust and spring pollen, and flies were lighting on my arms that were supporting Noah. I couldn't let go to itch or shoo as we walked briskly through the dirt and manure. Noah was oblivious to anything other than his horse and the bump-bumping rhythm of the ride; he was enjoying every moment.

Jeri gave directions from the center of the ring for the class. We walked around barrels so Noah could practice steering. The class progressed with a game of musical horse chairs. From a fence post, an old boom box with a cassette tape played squeaky kid music. The rider closest to the barrel when the music stopped continued to ride, while others stood off to the side on their horses. Noah was lucky at this game, and we walked around and around the ring until we were the last people and horse standing. My arm was numb, and I imagined my face looked like an old photo of a coal miner, black with dust, just my eyes showing. I assumed we were about done with the lesson. I felt done.

"Who wants to trot?" Jeri asked.

"Me!" volunteered Noah with more voice volume than I had ever heard from him, ever.

"Okay then," she said. I secretly hoped Jeri would think Noah wasn't ready to trot. I was not ready. "Walk your horse down to the other end of the ring, and when I give the command, trot your horse back," she said.

Fred, Noah and I, along with a few other riders, made our way down to the end of the ring. We checked Noah's stirrups; both of his feet were dangling off to the side. "I don't think it really matters," Fred said. "His feet are going to fall out anyway. We just need to hold him on and run with the horse."

"Okay. Are you ready Noah?" called Jeri.

"Ready!" he said.

Jeri gave us the order to commence, "Trot on!"

Red Man must have known this was the last hurrah and he hauled. Running alongside a horse while holding fifty pounds of slipping bouncing kid was no easy feat. Fred huffed and puffed along (he would have a heart attack a year later), and Red Man recalled his youth and ran like Seabiscuit. At the end of the ring, Red Man stopped hard, and Noah pitched into his mangy mane.

"That was fun!" Noah said. "Can we do it again?"

"Maybe next week," Fred said. I was pleased with his response.

Fred and I dismounted Noah from Red Man and we wheeled into the barn with the blanket and saddle to gather the post-ride grooming implements. Noah carefully brushed Red Man and whispered to the old horse, "I love you."

We loaded up the wheelchair into the van. Noah sat up front with me.

"Can we go again?" he asked.

"Sure. We'll go next week. You have six weeks of lessons."

"I like riding Red Man," Noah said.

All during the week Noah talked about his riding lesson and about "my horse Red Man." We made up stories about him and imagined what he was doing while we were eating supper or getting ready for bed.

"Maybe he's taking a shower, too," I teased.

"Horses don't take showers," Noah said.

"Are you sure?"

"They don't have hands," he said.

"True enough."

We returned the next week to ride, and Mike came along to help with the lesson. As we wandered through the barn, I noticed that Red Man wasn't around. The last trot Noah took on him was, in fact, his last. He'd died during the week, Jeri quietly told us. "He'll be riding a new horse, Chase," she said. I concealed Red Man's death from Noah.

"Where's Red Man?" he asked.

"Oh…he's sleeping. You'll be riding Chase today," I said.

"I want to ride Red Man."

"Not today. Come on. Let's get the stuff. We have to get Chase brushed up."

Noah combed and brushed Chase with the same affection he had offered Red Man the prior week. Chase was as dusty and hairy as Red Man.

"Wow. This is really a lot of dust and stuff," Mike said as he waved his hand in front of his face and blew the dander away. He and I lifted Noah onto Chase and off we went, holding him tight, so he could walk, play games and trot in the name of therapy.

We took Noah for riding lessons every spring and fall for several years. The experience remained dusty and hairy. I envied parents who could sit idly by on bleachers watching their able-bodied kids play soccer or softball, while reading a book or doing a crossword puzzle. We never got to the point of relaxing while Noah had his riding lessons. Noah got better at staying upright on his own; sometimes Mike and I could balance him with just one hand each. That was good progress in terms of therapy, but mostly the riding lessons were for the sake of fun. Noah learned to steer Chase around the ring well enough to force us to step into piles of horse poop, something that always made him laugh.

chapter 10 | Special Needs

Outside the Green Parrot in Key West.

Flying

Mike carried Noah onto the airplane. It was easier and faster than the skinny tall aisle wheelchair that we called the *Hannibal Lechter* seat. He carted him like an armload of wood, close to his chest, holding him high above the seat backs. Noah's sneakered foot would get caught sometimes.

"Legs in!" Mike said, and Noah tucked his legs closer to his dad as they progressed to our assigned seats.

We always boarded airplanes with first class passengers and other high mileage frequent fliers. I found it to be ironic when the announcement would come, "We're now boarding our first class passengers, people with small children and people with disabilities or anyone needing extra time with boarding." People with disabilities and little kids are pretty much second-class citizens in most other situations. In the days of unfilled airline flights, once in a while a compassionate attendant would offer us open first class seats. We'd nod knowingly to passengers proceeding to coach class as we sipped beers and nibbled nuts.

When we flew, usually to Florida, it was to escape the icy grey Michigan winters. We'd sit three across: Noah in the window seat, tiny compared to his six-foot plus dad; Mike in the center; and me on the aisle. Mike preferred the window seat, but from the center seat he could put his arm behind our son's back, so he could lean over him. Together with their faces close, they looked at the tiny American landscapes—fields white from snow turning to green and brown squares—and the tops of clouds below the bright blue sky.

Dolphins

The room was dim and air conditioner damp-cool in the small building that doubled as a micro-auditorium for the Dolphin Research Center. Hurricane shutters closed out all but bright slivers of light inside, and the scent was musty and humid, like most closed-up buildings in the tropics. This was such a radical change from the blazing white light and intense afternoon heat of the Florida Keys, just outside the door. Noah clutched the fin of the stuffed toy dolphin in his lap and listened carefully to the trainer.

"Be careful not to touch their eyes or the blow hole, and be gentle when you touch their noses. The nose is quite sensitive. When you grip on the dorsal fin, try to hold it with even pressure and don't pinch or grab it," she said. Noah spread his fingers across the plush fin, doing his best not to pinch the training toy.

"The skin of a dolphin isn't slippery, though it looks like it could be. It actually feels smooth and kind of like rubber. The water makes it a bit slick, but you'll be able to hold on just fine; I'll be there to help you," she said. Noah nodded.

The Dolphin Research Center in Grassy Key, Florida, provided a home and care for rescued dolphins and their offspring. For various reasons, these animals could not be returned to the wild, so they lived in open water enclosures on the Gulf side of the island. The center did behavioral research with the animals and provided opportunities for people to interact with the dolphins, including a "special needs" encounter program that gave one-on-one instruction and assistance to people with disabilities.

After a short video and a few questions, we pushed Noah outside to the dock. The air temperature was in the mid 80s, but the water was bit chilly, in the high 70s. With little body fat, cold water made Noah miserable. We opted to put him in a wetsuit for his dolphin swim encounter.

"This is going to be some fun," I said.

Noah sat in his chair watching the dolphins while Mike and I worked the black, neoprene suit onto him. At least his skinniness made the job a little easier.

Noah's limbs were long and gangly and his involuntary reflexes made dressing him like a wrestling match. His arms and legs would sometimes react without warning—freeing themselves from a sleeve or a half put-on pant leg. Occasionally, one of us would take an accidental whack to the ear or nose if we got too close when he thrashed. The excitement of dolphins jumping out of the water nearby, trainers blowing whistles, and people clapping added to Noah's normal spastic reactions made us shake our heads and laugh at the trial of dressing our son in a wetsuit.

"It smells kind of moldy," I said quietly about the suit the center provided.

"Ha! Everything in Florida smells like something funky," Mike said.

With one of us on each side, we worked one of Noah's long relaxed feet down the leg of the suit. His feet were sweating and kept getting stuck in the material.

"Ouch," he said, faking pain.

"Sorry about that Noah. Maybe if you paid attention and helped us a little, your toes wouldn't get caught," I said, slightly annoyed at his lack of focus on the task. He was looking off at the crisp blue and turquoise of the Gulf of Mexico and wasn't offering any help in getting dressed.

After about twenty minutes of trying, we got the suit up to his knees.

"Time to stand up," Mike said grabbing Noah around the chest and hoisting him up to standing on the foot rests of the wheelchair. Noah had the ability to bear his weight and stand, but had no balance. He was like a noodle in the middle, legs and arms that were strong enough, but zero core strength. Noah held onto Mike and I pulled the sleeveless (a small blessing) wetsuit up and worked on getting his arms through the holes.

"Done. He's in. Let me zip it," I said, as I reached a hand between Noah and Mike and finished the task. He looked handsome and happy in the black wetsuit. We rolled him to the dock and snapped a life vest on him

"I'm ready!" said Noah loudly to no one in particular, and everyone within earshot.

I jumped in the salty, tepid water first and Mike lowered Noah down. He bobbed on the surface of the water while the trainers got organized with their toys, fishy treats and other props. He laughed and splashed me pretending it was an accident. Splash. "Sorry. Mom." Splash. "Whoops."

"Have any of you kissed a dolphin before?" asked the trainer on the dock.

"I have!" Noah blurted. Then, more quietly, "Not really."

Two dolphins, AJ and Santini, were swimming around the enclosure. When the trainer whistled, Santini swam up to Noah, whom I'd placed in the arms and care of the special needs trainer.

She showed Noah how to gently pat the nose, helped hold his arm out straight to pet the dolphin as she swam by and cued him on when to give the kiss. Without reservation and with no real need for instruction, Noah laid a long kiss on its nose. The dolphin clicked happily and swam off.

Disney

"Here comes Goofy again. What is he anyway? A dog, or something else? He's not right," Mike said. We had to practically shoo the Disney characters away.

"I like Goofy," Noah said, so we paused to let the undetermined creature catch up with us.

Throughout Walt Disney World, at every turn, characters greeted us with enthusiasm—like we were old friends. If they were talking characters, we'd engage in idle, polite conversation. Chip and Dale along with multiple Goofies, Mickey, Minnie, Eeyore, Captain Hook, Cinderella, Pooh, Piglet, Tigger, Pluto, Snow White and most of the Seven Dwarves sought time with Noah. One would start coming toward us and we'd slow down, stop, chat, move on. Then as we moved just around the corner we'd come upon another character. This was a fundamental change from our normal life. People with disabilities are literally overlooked—people don't want to look them in the eye, they look around, beyond or above—as if eye contact was *verboten*. If they did notice him, people usually gawked and looked away quickly; here, at Disney World, though, the characters were interacting with him and coming to us with purpose and intention. I tried to act cool and aloof like a celebrity might when a fan approaches, but I was secretly pleased because Noah was delighted with the attention. Instead of being accidently excluded, he was being purposefully included.

"Take a picture, Mom." These were pre-digital camera days and I was blowing through roll after roll of film, but I couldn't say no to my happy kid at the happiest place on earth.

A young boy in a wheelchair, with knobby knees, curly blonde hair and a few missing front teeth is a character magnet. Characters stopped whatever they were doing and made a beeline for Noah.

Snow White was happily talking to a crowd of little girls when she spotted Noah. She politely excused herself and hurried over to greet him.

"Well, hello! Welcome to Disney World. Are you having a fun visit? What's your name?" she asked in a gentle princess-y voice.

Noah was dazzled and speechless. Finally after a long minute, he squeezed out his name, barely audible. He thought she was cute.

"Noah."

Snow White leaned closer. "I'm afraid I didn't hear you," she said kindly.

"Noah," he repeated with more volume.

"It's nice to meet you, Noah. Would you like to have your picture taken with me?"

"Mom, take our picture, please," he said.

I got out the camera. Snow White's arm was around the top of Noah's chair, and she crouched a bit so their faces were even. Noah's expression was blissful as I snapped it. "Thank you Noah, for letting me be in your picture," she said bidding us farewell, returning to the able-bodied little girls who were waiting in the hot Florida sun for their turn to be special.

Good Seats

For Noah's thirteenth birthday, we bought tickets to see Jimmy Buffett at a big pavilion near Chicago for the *2001: A Beach Odyssey* tour. It was Noah's first concert and he was excited—he'd been listening to and singing Buffett songs with us since he was a toddler and it seemed like the right age for a concert. We'd opted for a Thursday night show on September 13, just ten days before his birthday. That specific show never happened.

Later in the month, as people were still reeling, but trying to be normal again after the 9/11 attacks, the show was rescheduled. We drove to Tinley Park outside Chicago but didn't hang out in the parking lot with the other Parrotheads. We were still edgy and cautious after the attacks and opted to get into our seats and have a beer. The previously sold out show was now less filled. It was a cool night, temperatures were in the 50s—the Midwestern autumn had arrived. We wore jackets over our Hawaiian shirts and leis and we fashioned bandanas as pirate hats to keep warm.

As a security guard guided us to our seats in the disabled seating section, he made a diversion. "Come with me," he said. We followed. He led us to the front row for the show. "This will be more fun for you and your son," he said.

"Thanks," I said. We'd never had front row seats before. Folding chairs were lined in rows and there was a big gap between the first row and the stage. We were on the left end of the stage, not front and center, but close enough.

The show was more subdued than a normal Jimmy Buffett concert. It was only the second show after the 9/11 attacks. Jimmy talked with the audience about tolerance, kindness, taking care of one another. He opened with the song, "Only Time Will Tell." Noah and I danced through most of the first set in the space in front of the stage, spinning his wheelchair back and forth and around in circles to the music. I'm sure I knocked my shin with the footplate as I usually did with wheelchair dancing. Dancing with someone in a wheelchair looks possible and fun in the mind's eye, but in reality it is awkward and un-rhythmic. He laughed as I swung him in circles and together we sang songs like "Brown Eyed Girl" and "Cheeseburger in Paradise."

Just after the intermission, Jimmy sang one of Noah's favorite songs—"Jolly Mon Sing" and Mike put Noah on his shoulders for a better view. Noah gripped his dad's head, transfixed by the live music and the lights. After the song ended, a crewmember motioned to us, leaned over the edge of the stage gave Noah one of Jimmy's guitar picks.

We believed that Jimmy himself spotted Noah on his dad's shoulders and sent it over.

Chairs

There were five wheelchairs in Noah's lifetime. One was green, another purple, two were blue and the last was red. He chose his chair colors carefully, as one would for a new car or a first bike. The green chair was his first, the blues represented his favorite colors at the time, the purple one was metallic and very mature-looking, and red was the color of Muskegon High School. Those chairs brought him to the world. His chair got him to the bus for school. It took him to the altar for communion at Mass. It helped him spend the summer at camp. He could roll through the woods, down a dock or out on an iced-over lake. In his chair he could stroll around museums and look at art or skeletons. His chair parted crowds on busy city streets and got us good seats.

Noah was never wheelchair bound—he was wheelchair freed.

chapter 11 | Noah Finds Us a Daughter

Our adoption day family photo.

Noah knew Tasha before we did. Even before we thought about becoming her foster parents, they were connected. When I made visits to Noah's classroom for special events or just to have lunch, Tasha would hang around us. Her clothes were dirty, and they usually didn't fit right, and they never matched. She had dark circles under her eyes and would race around the room, from one thing to another, becoming easily distracted. She was unbearably cute with big brown eyes and pale, almost translucent skin, wide forehead, chipmunk cheeks and an impish sense of play. She was born in Pikeville, Kentucky (home territory of the feudin' Hatfield and McCoy families) and she had been brought up to Muskegon as a baby. She spoke with some of the worst grammar I'd ever heard with a rural Kentucky accent.

"I'm about to be" was a common preface to anything she was doing or thinking of doing. "I'm about to be mad" or "I'm about to be goin' to the bus stop." Despite years of speech therapy for this and other speech issues, she never lost this odd trait.

One of the first times I saw her, she was dressed up, wearing a purple and white pinstripe dress with sleeves that covered her hands. The-two-sizes-too-big dress went below her knees, and she was wearing white high top sneakers, which also looked too big for her feet. She had on worn and snagged tights that were supposed to be white, but were actually grey. She was, despite her ragamuffin clothing, as cute as any little girl I'd ever seen. I wanted to fix her up.

When she was a baby, her mother and father gave her to her grandmother to be raised because they felt they couldn't do the job. They also brought the grandmother two sons, one older than Tasha and another younger. Her grandmother, a coalminer's daughter, had only a fifth grade education. She was no more able to raise Tasha and her brothers than her parents were. It wasn't a structured, healthy or happy upbringing. Her grandmother didn't talk or read to Tasha. She didn't feed her well or provide anything to help her develop socially or cognitively. Whether it was from genetics, neglect or some of both, she was left with a very low IQ. Child development science tells us that the first three years are the most important in a child's life for cognitive development. Tasha missed out on those first critical three years and five more after that. She came to our house and we did the best we could to teach, guide and love her. Some of it worked and much of it did not.

During her first year with us, Tasha told us that in her "old house" she often slept on the floor covered with a jacket. She suffered from asthma and frequent head lice. "I had to get food from the garbage can," she once confessed. When we read her Protective Services files we learned that the family moved often and had no refrigerator or stove in their last apartment. Her neglect was "severe" and caseworkers strongly suspect she was sexually abused, probably from her grandmother's brothers or boyfriends.

We could see early on that Noah was her friend and she was his protector. Tasha was strong, energetic and athletic, and she loved helping Noah. She was the one who volunteered to push him in his wheelchair to the library, the gym or down to the office on an errand for the teacher. She hung around Noah in class whenever she could. He wasn't very skilled (or fast) at moving his wheelchair and he needed help getting his jacket, hat and mittens on in winter. This gave Tasha a role. She was always eager to help him and took offense when other kids tried to intervene.

"No! I'm about to be helping Noah. He's my friend," she said one day as I observed her in the classroom. Whatever Noah needed or wanted she was ready to give to him.

We have a photograph from one of those early school days. The class was on a field trip to the winter sports complex in North Muskegon. Tasha and another girl are wearing ice skates, Tasha's ankle turned in slightly because it was the first time she'd ever worn them. The whole class is lined up at the edge of the rink with two other girls in wheelchairs and Noah in his. The laps and legs of the wheelchair kids are wrapped in blankets. Tasha is standing closest to Noah, and she's the only one not wearing a hat. Her hair is very short and uneven all over her head. From the looks of it, she hacked it off herself with scissors, or perhaps someone else in the family did the job. She's pale, tiny and wearing a dirty purple snow jacket. She is, though, smiling happily, as is Noah.

❖

A year before we met Tasha, we'd applied to become foster parents. I had read the book *White Oleander,* which gave me the impetus to act on an idea I'd been harboring. The foster daughter in the book was so further neglected and abused by foster families that I knew I could do a better job than those fictional characters. I'd been longing to parent a daughter for a few years, and felt like I had something in me to give to another child. Besides, as Noah grew into adolescence, he became closer to Mike. They seemed to need me less; they'd foray out on their own to places unknown to me for entire afternoons. "Where'd you guys go?" I'd ask when they'd return and all I'd get back would be a cagey reply from one or the other, "Here and there. Down by Grand Haven and Holland." They liked hanging out with one another, and I wasn't always invited.

With Noah's special needs, we couldn't take a whole family of foster kids, so when we applied, we specified a daughter. She had to be younger than Noah with no siblings. Most kids in foster care don't come in singles. They're removed from the home and like Tasha, there are usually two or three. A whole year went by and we only fostered one girl, a thirteen-year-old who stayed for a month and then moved on to a relative's house.

We'd pretty much given up on being foster parents when someone mentioned to me (with a *don't let anyone know where you heard this but...*) that Tasha had been removed from her grandmother's home because of an incident at school. One winter day, a strange man came to pick Tasha up after school.

"I don't think we've met," said her teacher to the man.

"The kid's momma is in a nursing home. Had to have her toe cut off," he said.

"And you are?"

"I'm her boyfriend," he said. "I bet Tasha was tired today. She was kicking and thrashin' me all night last night."

The teacher took a deep breath, helped Tasha zip her coat and called Children's Protective Services. Tasha and her two brothers went to an emergency shelter, and then a foster family. When I'd heard this, I called our caseworker.

"We'd love to take in Tasha. We know that she's at Child Haven right now. I think all of our licensing is up-to-date," I said, proving our readiness.

"We're trying to keep Tasha and her two brothers together. It's just better for siblings to be together," she said. "If there is some reason for a split, you'll be the first call I make," she said. I prayed and hoped that she would come live with us. I knew we could provide a good and stable home for her. We could help get her healthy and caught up on her learning and social skills. Above all, I knew we could love her.

After a month had passed and I was certain Tasha would not be coming to live with us, our social worker called. The dynamic between Tasha and her brothers was at odds with what the foster mom thought was normal. They seemed to always beat up on one another, were overly physical, sometimes sexually acting out with one another and something was just *not right*. The mom thought that Tasha was at the heart of the awkward dynamic and without her, the two boys would probably be better able to function. We agreed to take Tasha.

"Noah," I said over supper. "Tasha from school needs a place to live. Her family isn't taking good care of her. Dad and I think we can help. What do you think of that?"

"Hmm," said Noah. "Hmm" meant he was thinking.

After a pause, he simply said, "Okay."

"It will be different to have someone else around, a sister. A girl. Mom and Dad will have to give her attention, too," I told him.

Noah didn't say anything. We helped him eat his supper. After a few minutes he asked, "How long will she stay?"

"I don't know. I think for a few months, maybe more. There are some problems with her family that they're going to try to fix. Until then, she'll stay with us. You can have a sister. That will be fun, won't it?" I asked.

"Maybe," Noah said.

The next day the foster family appeared with Tasha and a garbage bag half full of wadded clothing, balled up socks, an old blanket, three pairs of worn out shoes and a newish fake American Girl doll.

"Noah!" she screamed, her face lit with a smile as she hugged him tight. She seemed surprised to see him. She'd forgotten, or never fully understood, that she was coming to live with Noah and us. Noah looked skeptical.

"I'm about to be living here?" she said.

"Yes, if you like it, you can stay," I said.

"I like it. I'll stay."

She roamed around the house looking into the rooms and meeting our dog, Murphy. She squeezed him hard. We showed her the room that would be hers and promised to paint it and make it hers if she decided to stay. I wanted her to feel like she had a choice in the living arrangement.

"I'm stayin'. Noah can be my brother," she said with conviction.

Noah didn't say anything, other than "Hmm."

And so she stayed. She became part of our family and a year later we adopted her.

From the beginning, we knew Tasha had the capacity for love. The love she had for Noah was the only honest and true love she had ever known and reciprocated. She loved him tenderly and with care. He never did anything to harm her, nor she him. As her parents, we were the rule-makers and structure people. I had to say "no" to her far more times than I said "yes."

Noah's death was another one of her many abandonments. To a girl who never knew her real parents, was given up by her grandmother and separated from her biological brothers, abandonment was the one thing she knew something about. Noah's death was another abandonment. She loved Noah and when she talked about him, even after he was gone, she would tear up and cry. She often talked about being with him in heaven, and when she was very sad, she would say she wanted to be with him right away.

When Noah died, some part of Mike and me died, too. Our family lost its focal point. Tasha came to us because of Noah. With him gone, we were more like three separate individuals living in the same home than a connected family; Noah had been that connection for all of us. Mike and I were so full of grief that we had a hard time trying to keep a normal-appearing life for the other child in our life. And she was needy for that attention. Loving Tasha was hard because we loved and missed Noah so much.

We plodded forward as a broken family. She became wary of initiating talk about Noah, as it would make me cry. Her questions would come out at unexpected times; she'd just think of something and blurt it. "If Noah is really in heaven, then why are his ashes upstairs?" or "Remember when we took Noah up to camp and you cried in the van?" She didn't intend to be hurtful; this was just her way of sorting things out, curious about death. I wasn't ready to answer her questions or talk about it. I didn't want to spend my grief energy on her when I had my own feelings to sort through. We found her a psychologist to talk with and sent her to a camp for grieving children, but I'm sure that what she could not articulate was that she was being emotionally pushed aside as we tended to our loss.

Our bond with Tasha had a late start. We didn't know her as a baby. We never got to see any of her "firsts"—by the time she came to us she could already ride a two-wheeler and insisted she needed no help in the shower. There were no first steps, smiles, or "Mama" or "Da." I never changed her diapers, never gave her a bath, tied her shoes, dressed, or fed her. We never held her hand as she crossed the street to start her first day of school. We have only a few photographs of her before the age of eight. The story of her birth was as much a mystery as her ethnicity.

Our emotional history was short and lacked the depth that both parents and children deserve. She was never an affectionate child, not to us anyway. The abuse and neglect inflicted made her wary of relationships with adults, especially parent figures, since it was adults who did her harm. We were mostly her caregivers and providers. She really never bonded with anyone besides Noah. The two brothers that she was separated from when she went into foster care have all but disappeared. If she mentioned them it was not more than once or twice a year, and without any longing or connection. Her sibling connection was with Noah alone.

Despite the fact she is our daughter and we love her as best we are able, I sometimes feel that I'm not totally and completely her mother—and without Noah, the feeling of not being a mother to anyone anymore is compounded.

I think of myself as being a mother in past tense.

I was a mother.

chapter 12 | Suspended Belief

Noah, the model student.

J ust before lunch the phone on my desk rang. The caller
   ID read: *Muskegon Pub Sch.* It was familiar; I got frequent
   calls from school to field a question from one of Noah's
teachers, his aide or the physical or speech therapist. Sometimes
Noah would call to tell me he'd aced a test and to name his reward.
I picked up the receiver.

"Missus King?" The voice on the line was unfamiliar. "This is
the secretary at Marquette School. You need to come pick Noah
Miesch up at school."

"What's going on? Is he okay?" I wasn't too concerned. When
Noah took a spill or hurt himself the call came from his aide,
Kitty, or his teacher, Julie.

"Noah has been suspended for three days," she said.

Three days! What could he have done? He's a kid in a wheelchair.
Racing thoughts were clogging my mouth. *Really, what could it be?
A knife? Where would he get a knife? Swearing? Could they suspend
him for three days for saying "dammit"? Noah's never done anything
really bad… What? What?*

"Missus King, Noah pulled the fire alarm."

I gasped and then I smiled. *Oh, Noah.*

"No kidding. Wow. When do I have to get him?"

"Right now. He's waiting in the office."

When I called Mike, he was as shocked as I was. I told him
what the secretary said. He was quiet for a moment and then said,
"I can't believe Noah could do that."

Not "would," but "could." Noah's cerebral palsy left him with little
fine motor control. He could feed himself, slowly and awkwardly.
He might be able to pull a zipper up if it had something on it to

make the task easier. He could move his power wheelchair around with a joystick, but he couldn't move a manual chair by its wheels. His hands were often clenched fists. Periodic Botox injections would help loosen them, but his hand control was limited. The fire alarm seemed like a mighty task.

Mike and I pulled into the school parking lot at the same time and walked into the office together. It was early December and Noah was sitting in the office looking concerned and guilty. He was wearing his dark green L.L. Bean jacket. The hood was up and his nose looked sweaty. The school must have been expecting us to arrive sooner than we did.

"Wow, Noah, you're in some big trouble," I said sternly.

Noah looked at his boots and said, "That was bad."

"Sure was," said Mike flipping Noah's hood off as the secretary presented us with a short stack of papers to sign. "You need to call the fire department, too. Here's the number," she said.

"Really, three days?" I took the papers from the secretary.

"Yes ma'am. Pulling a fire alarm is a three-day suspension. It is very serious."

"Yes, it is serious," I said glancing at Noah and giving him *the* look. "I agree. It just seems like three days is kind of harsh, kind of long." I was thinking of how we would manage this and who would take time off, Mike or me?

"Can we talk with Mrs. Johns?" Mike said. Mike and Mrs. Johns, the school principal, had taken art classes together in college. She greeted Mike with a long hug and led us into her office. We pleaded for leniency.

"Noah does seem remorseful. I talked with him after he pulled the alarm and he said he was sorry—he had tears in his eyes. He's been very quiet in here," Mrs. Johns said looking past us into the outer office at Noah. She gave him a reduced sentence of two days, including this day, much to our relief.

We thanked her and she escorted us out, saying a few kind words to Noah. We wheeled him out of the school, his chair marking the snowy parking lot with parallel tracks.

"Noah, what were you thinking?" I said.

"I don't know," Noah said.

"Of course you know. Why did you do such a thing? You knew full well that pulling the fire alarm was wrong."

"I know."

"You know you're in some big trouble don't you?"

"I'm sorry," said Noah.

"I know you're sorry Noah, but sorry doesn't make up for the whole school evacuating on a cold winter day, and the fire department coming to the school for nothing. This is very bad." I paused and then I pulled the *Santa card*. He was twelve years old and still a Santa believer. We'd never discouraged it and helped build the myth. Over the last few Christmases, I'd developed the *One Hundred Presents* discipline strategy, which involved telling Noah that Santa had a hundred presents for him just waiting to be loaded onto the sleigh. But every time Noah swore, refused to be helpful, was defiant, did poorly on a test he'd studied for or did something not nice, Santa reduced the load by one present. If he were lucky, we told him, by Christmas he would have twenty or so presents under the tree.

"Santa is not going to be happy about this," I said. "I think it will cost you about twenty-five presents."

"Dammit."

"Ooh, that's another present."

"I hate Santa," Noah mumbled.

"Ooh. That's pretty serious," said Mike. "All you're going to get for Christmas is underwear."

Noah swore again.

Mike loaded him and his chair into the van, and they headed home to spend the afternoon together. Noah remained crabby and quiet. His dad wouldn't let him watch television, so he lay on his big purple floor pillow, his "nest" as we called it, and looked at books, messed with toys and played with Murphy.

When I came home, Tasha was beside herself with happiness. Though she was five years younger than Noah, they shared a multi-age Special Ed classroom, and she was the one who was always in trouble.

"Mom! Mom, did you hear what Noah did?" She was dancing at the doorway.

"I heard something about…" She interrupted me. I was trapped in the kitchen listening to her version of the story. "He pulled the alarm at school and we all had to go outside and it was cold and we weren't wearing jackets and the fire trucks came and we all had to stand on the sidewalk and I saw Mr. Art from next door and Noah had to go to the office and was suspended," she said.

"Wow. That was something. Were you outside for long?" I said.

"Like maybe a half hour or an hour. It was a long time and we were cold. Are you going to whip Noah?" I detected hope in her voice.

"Have we ever whipped Noah? Or you?" I tried not to laugh.

"No. But Noah pulled the fire alarm." She was clearly trying to convince me he needed a whipping.

"Shut up," Noah said from the living room.

"Noah just told me to shut up," Tasha said.

"Asshole!" Noah shouted.

"Okay, Tasha, stop talking about the fire alarm. Now. Noah, stop with the swearing. Now."

"But Mom, Noah pulled the alarm and swore at me. Isn't he in trouble?"

"Yes, he's been suspended and can't go to school tomorrow or Monday."

I could see her forehead wrinkle as she thought. "He pulled the alarm and gets to stay home with you?"

"I know, it seems wrong to you, but that's what's happening. You go to school and he stays home."

"Not fair," said Tasha.

"No kidding."

Dinner was quiet. Occasionally, Tasha would disclose some detail about the incident, which would cause Noah to curse or tell her to shut up. Because they were in the same classroom, she felt like an insider and was eager to throw Noah under the bus for his malfeasance.

I read to them before bed, Noah lying in his twin bed and Tasha wrapped in a blanket on the end. I searched the bookshelf looking for something that involved a fire truck, but they were both a bit old for that. I read *Per and the Dala Horse*, a Swedish folktale that felt somewhat Christmas-like. Per resembled Noah in the illustrations, and I liked that.

I kissed Tasha, and she went off to her bedroom across the hall. I tucked Noah in under his sailboat quilt and kissed him, too.

"Tomorrow will be a better day."

"Mom? I'm sorry," Noah said.

"I know you are. Everything will be okay. Don't worry too much," I said as I tried to smooth a wrinkle from his brow. The concerned look on his face was adorable.

"Sleep tight, love."

After the kids were asleep and Mike and I went to bed, we finally had a chance to talk. We whispered so the kids in their rooms below us couldn't hear.

"I can't believe he did it," I said.

"Me, either. I didn't think he had the hand coordination or strength," Mike said.

"Who do you think parked his chair so close to the alarm? He didn't wheel over there himself."

"I've always said he had a praying mantis reflex. He sees something, gets his focus and makes one fast grab for it and usually makes it," Mike said. This was true. Noah would eye a ball on a pool table and could make a move for it, grabbing it with success. He took great delight in knocking a beer out of his Uncle Dick's hand.

"Pulling an alarm is serious, but I'm kind of proud of Noah," I said. "He's lived all his life with limited naughtiness. This was big for any kid and huge for Noah."

Doing things independently is the hallmark achievement of any kid with a disability—whether it's maneuvering a wheelchair, eating, participating in an activity or making a decision. Parents tend to "do" for their disabled kids, move them, get them things, make their decisions and limit their choices. This "doing" isn't always intentional—it's just easier. Over time, kids with disabilities like Noah have what is called *learned dependence*. There were things that Noah could do, but chose not to, because he knew if he waited long enough or refused, we'd give in and do it for him. He was able to feed himself. He proved it at camp each summer, but at home, he let us feed him. It was faster, less messy and he could eat more food with us controlling the fork. When Noah pulled the fire alarm, it was a moment of complete independence. He did it without help or permission from anyone.

❖

When I called the fire station in the morning, the officer seemed surprised.

"Normally, we talk with the kids at school after the incident and they go through a short program with us here at the station. But…" he paused. "Well, with Noah, being in a wheelchair and all… maybe we can skip that," said Major Metcalf.

Mike and I made sure in bringing up Noah that his disability wasn't used as an excuse not to participate in life's activities. If a meeting with someone from the fire department was what alarm-pulling kids did, then Noah would do it, too.

"Wait. If there is a program, he needs to do it," I said.

We arranged for a visit at noon.

Noah and I spent a quiet morning working on his schoolwork and practicing his spelling words. He was a model student and worked hard on the assignments I read to him. He could tell I was still annoyed about the incident.

I called his teacher Julie for details. "Noah had been eyeing the alarm all week," she said. "We told him to keep away, and he knew if he pulled it, he would get in trouble." An occupational therapy student was taking Noah to the OT room. When she went back to get something, he pulled the alarm. "It scared him half to death. He practically stood up in his wheelchair. Noah never expected it to be so loud and so sudden," she said.

My eyes filled with tears. I loved my naughty kid so much at that moment.

"He knew the minute he pulled it he was in trouble. I hated to turn him in, but I had to," she said. "I shouldn't tell you this, but we all were kind of proud that Noah was able to do it." I could hear the smile in her voice. "Just in case of a real fire, of course."

I bundled Noah into his green jacket and pulled up the hood as we headed to the old fire station in downtown Muskegon. I reminded Noah to watch his mouth and to listen carefully to the firefighter. "Answer any questions he might have and be respectful, Noah. No messing around."

"I promise."

Entering through the administration door, we were greeted by Major Metcalf. My mood improved. He was tall and handsome, with a great smile and a firm handshake. He and Noah sat at a table, and I sat off to the side where Noah couldn't see me, but I could see Major Metcalf.

"So Noah," he began. "Do you know why pulling a fire alarm is a bad thing?"

"Yes," he said. Then, "No, not really."

"Do you have a dog?"

"Yes."

"What's his name?" asked Major.

"Murphy."

"Do you love Murphy? Do you help take care of him?"

"Yes. I love him," squeaked Noah.

"Well, imagine, Noah, if there was a fire at your house and Murphy was in the house. And your mom called 911, but instead of being able to send a fire truck to your house, the truck was at the school for a false alarm. What might happen?"

Noah thought about this for a bit. "Murphy. Might. Die?" Noah said with a lump in his throat. Both he and the firefighter were silent.

"That's why, Noah, you can't pull the fire alarm. It could be your dog, or someone else's dog, house or even a family. Firefighters need to be ready and able to go to a fire fast. We can't be playing around with false alarms at schools."

"Okay. I'm sorry," said Noah. I came forward and put my arm around him.

"I think this was a good talk, Major. Thank you. What do you think Noah?"

"I won't do it again. I promise." His cheeks were damp with tears and I wiped them away.

We all shook hands, and Noah and I left the fire station.

"How about we get some lunch, Noah. Are you hungry?"

"Yes," he sniffled.

We left the fire station and headed to Carmen's, a little diner, where we were the only customers after the lunch rush. We ate buttery grilled cheese sandwiches and ordinary tomato soup—comfort food on a winter day just before Christmas.

chapter 13 | Love Regardless

Awkward pre-teens, Noah and Tasha.

tried to pluck it from him because I thought it was one of my stray curly hairs. I seem to lose a lot of them and they appear on my dark clothing, on our black car seats, between book pages and occasionally in food I've cooked.

Just after a shower, Mike carried Noah, who was swaddled in a big blue towel, from the shower chair in our bathroom to his bed, where I was waiting to put pajamas on him. I instinctively pulled on the hair down there. It was stuck.

"Ouch!" Noah said. The little blonde curly hair was his own, his first pube.

"Mike, come in here," I called. "You need to see this—Noah has a hair, several hairs, down there."

Noah winced and blushed. "Mom, don't…"

"I noticed it a while back," Mike said as he entered the room.

"And you didn't mention it, why?"

"I thought you already saw it. Saw them," he said as he tried not to laugh. "Before too long he'll have a pencil-thin moustache and a wife."

"I'm cold," Noah said, as he lay naked and still wet on the towel as we discussed facial hair and upcoming weddings.

When you dress and undress your child for years, you notice all sorts of things. Noah had a dark mole on his left butt cheek and for fun, we called him *moldy butt*. Sometimes when Mike carried him over his shoulder, like a bag of charcoal briquettes, from shower to bedroom, he'd stop, unveil Noah's moldy butt, and I'd give it a gentle slap. Laughing, Noah would warn us, "Butt splash!" as if his butt was so wet it would splash water on our faces.

Most parents don't have to bathe their kids or see them naked after they're done with elementary school. But, kids with severe disabilities, especially those with mobility issues, rely on their parents or other people for personal care throughout their lives. Noah, because of his cerebral palsy was no different in the care he needed at three, ten or seventeen years old. Despite his disability, we never thought of him as helpless. He told us what he wanted and what he was thinking. He had opinions and ideas, but, without our help, he couldn't execute his physical intentions. As his parents and caregivers, we were part of his private moments, as well as the everyday tasks that most people don't think about.

Parents understand the organization needed to venture out with a baby. With a disabled child, the organization grows and becomes more complicated as the years pass. Kids become teens and they get bigger, heavier and taller, but often need the same help as they did when they were younger. We became expert life planners. I'd always imagined that Mike and I were hippie-like people, free and easy-going, but the reality is, we might have been at one time, but by the time Noah was five, we were not. Our skill in being structured crept up on us, almost like the severity of Noah's disability.

For normal sorts of activities, like going to Mass, we needed to structure in small amounts of additional time. Noah needed to get into his jacket, settled into his wheelchair, out of the house, down the ramp, onto the van lift, buckled and strapped into the van and then get the lift folded back into the van. At the church, we needed extra time to unbuckle and unstrap Noah's wheelchair, lower the lift, remove Noah from the lift, fold the lift back up, roll into the church to find a pew with an empty space on the end so Noah could sit next to me, since church pews don't quite accommodate wheelchairs. We needed extra space to turn him around to get to the back of the church and get up the aisle for communion.

We didn't leave the house without a plan. Accessibility was always a concern—would there be steps? If so, how many? We could handle a few, but taking his chair up a flight or two wasn't safe or easy, though we did it more than once. Before we chose a restaurant, we checked out the seating and the bathrooms— we needed a table, not a booth or a high top, and a bathroom without barriers.

Part of the structure of our life was getting Noah up and moving in the morning. Sometimes, even when he was in high school we'd sneak into his room together, throw on the lights and sing, with motions, an old Girl Scout camp song. We sang the words loudly, startling Noah awake.

Way up in the sky,
the big birds fly,
while down in the nest the little birds rest.
With a wing on the left and a wing on the right,
the little birds sleep all through the night.
Shh, they're sleeping.
The bright sun comes up,
the dew falls away,
Good morning! Good morning! the little birds say.

Every single day we dressed him—unless he was in wake and wear, a clothing combination of plaid flannel pants from Beans

and a long or short sleeve t-shirt that could be worn for pajamas
and to school. He needed his ankle foot orthotics strapped on,
which required a few minutes of foot stretching. He also wore
a splint on his clenched and tight right hand. It gave him more
range of motion and flexibility. Nothing with Noah was fast, easy
or uncomplicated.

Mike usually fed Noah breakfast while I dressed for
work. When they were done eating, I came in with a hot, wet
washcloth to de-crustify his face and brush his teeth. "Ouch!
You're hurting me," Noah said, thrashing away from me as I
attempted to wipe sleep from his eyes or remove egg matter
from around his mouth. Moving through the morning routine,
the next stop was the toilet (a large potty chair over the toilet
with a big belt that Velcroed around his waist) where we put
him and where he sat captive until one of us came to get him.
Sometimes he told us he had to go, other times we just put
him there when the time seemed right, like in the morning. It
was all part of our rigid organization. Neither of us wanted our
teenage son pooping his pants.

"I'm done. I pooped," he called out. "Come get me!"

"Are you sure?" I'd tease him from outside the door.

"I'm sure."

"You better be sure," I said.

Mike and I sometimes debated who would do the wipe and
toilet dismount. It usually depended on who was running ahead
or behind schedule that morning.

Leaning Noah forward onto the toilet, I'd have a wad of paper
in my hand to wipe his butt.

"There's no poop in there," I said looking into the bowl.

"Just kidding," Noah said. "I'll poop at school."

"That's weird, you're a school pooper."

Noah laughed at the idea of being a school pooper.

As a toddler, he could feed himself—not really well, but good enough. By the time he was three, the tone and spasms in his hands and arms increased and he began to fling food or poke himself in the face with a fork.

"Come on Noah," we coached. "Steady does it." We guided his arm, hand and fork toward his mouth. We tried to feed him things that would stick on a fork. Chunks of cheese, scrambled eggs, macaroni and individual peas worked well.

"I can do it," he said and then the idea, the excitement of success kicked in and his hand would spasm and off went the food. Meals with Noah feeding himself lasted at least an hour, and the food intake was minimal. So, we fed him when he was a toddler and when he was a teen. We never thought much about it or how it might look to others when we went out to eat. It was just normal to us.

Noah's hands were locked up, tight and fisted from the cerebral palsy. His involuntary movements made driving his wheelchair a stop-start-veer-halt-careen-start-again activity. Mike and I helped him steer because we didn't have the patience or the time to wait for him to amble along in his chair. Noah was a daydreamer and would set off for a destination, become distracted and angle off toward another place. So, we took control of the joystick of his power chair or pushed him from the back of a manual chair and moved him as needed.

For most of Noah's life it was the three of us. Tasha came into the family when Noah was thirteen years old and our highly structured routine was already established and comfortable. From what we'd heard about the needs of foster kids, structure was a plus for her success. We knew in addition to love, we had abundant structure.

Disability makes for a close family mostly because accessibility makes friendships for disabled kids difficult. If there are steps to a friend's home, or a playground isn't accessible, the kid in the wheelchair is likely to be left out. Even when there's a desire for inclusion, the logistics of moving a kid in a wheelchair without a specialized van is a challenge. We did as much picking up and dropping off as we were able, but it wasn't enough for Noah to develop the deep friendships that other kids enjoy as they become teenagers. That continual contact that kids have with one another from about middle school to high school just didn't exist for Noah. There were no sleepovers, video game hang outs, car rides, prep sports events, or dates for him. He had good friends in school, there were kids he talked about and socialized with during the day. He'd talk with kids on the phone sometimes, but after school and on weekends, it was just family. Mike and I were Noah's parents and his best friends. If it bothered him that he had no close friends, he never mentioned it or complained to us. Of course, we wished things were different for our son, but that kind of normal would never be our reality.

With disabled kids, there are degrees of very personal *stuff* parents have to deal with. For some people it is diapers and drooling, teenage daughters in wheelchairs with periods or cognitively-impaired boys masturbating without warning. We get used to and, eventually, sometimes uneasily accept whatever surprise our kids might bring us. The wide spectrum of human frailty, wrapped up in emotion and love is at the core of these special parent-child relationships.

Noah's disability shaped his character and personality and Noah's care and daily needs sharply defined our family dynamics, relationships, daily routines and rituals. This was even more so for Mike, especially when he reduced his work hours to part-time to care for Noah when he became ill.

"I was always just Noah's dad," he said. "That's how people knew me, that was my job. I lost some of that identity when he died."

chapter 14 | Noah Flies Off

A few of his favorite things.

sat quietly in the butter-yellow colored hospital room looking at the numbers on Noah's pulse oximeter. They were in the high 80s, not good when 99-100 is ideal. It was better than the high 70s of two days ago, though. I leafed through an issue of *The New Yorker*, which I'd grabbed from the mail pile as I left the house. The oxygen numbers rose and fell as he slept. I celebrated when they went up and worried when they dropped.

Noah was in the small pediatric unit of Mercy Hospital being treated for pneumonia. Up until this spring day, he'd been a healthy child and teen with no illness-related hospitalizations. We didn't know it then, but from this admission to his death he'd only have one more summer at camp, one more birthday and one more Christmas.

He'd been on the unit for a few days and wasn't improving or getting worse either. He was weak and pale. He wasn't coughing much, which was a problem because coughing was what pneumonia patients needed to do. I planned to ask his pediatrician about transferring him to the children's hospital— this peds unit was too quiet. I wanted a place with more sick kids and more kid medical experts.

I arrived at the hospital before 7 a.m., so I could talk with nurses from both shifts. They told me he had slept through the night and nothing much had changed.

An hour later, the food service cart stopped and a worker brought in a tray. The noise awoke Noah. He turned his head toward the noise, saw me and smiled. "Hi Mom. Where's Dad?"

"He's at work. He'll be in at noon. I bet he'll eat some of your lunch if you don't watch out. You have scrambled eggs and bacon for breakfast." The tray didn't look too bad. "There's chocolate milk, too."

"I'm not hungry," he said.

"How about a quick trip to the bathroom? You can eat later."

"I don't have to pee."

We watched television for a bit and messed with the balloons that decorated Noah's room. He liked balloons and every visitor brought him a few. Balloons were tied to the bed rails, taped to the windowsill and tied on the visitor chairs. When I had worked at Mercy, up until just six months before Noah's illness, I used to bring fun and festive Mylar balloons home from the hospital gift shop on any special occasion, like Valentine's Day, Halloween, or even just a Friday.

Noah coughed occasionally, but seemed listless and sad in contrast to the lively balloons. Out the window things were starting to green up. I could see spots of bright yellow—daffodils and dandelions were blooming on the hospital lawn. It was a sunny clear day, but I felt sad like Noah did.

He sipped some chocolate milk and ignored the rest of the breakfast tray.

"You've been up for an hour—it's time for a pee." He didn't argue, and I wheeled him into the bathroom. In the hospital there was no over-the-toilet potty chair like we had at home. I stood close as he sat and gripped my leg for support, like hugging a tree trunk. It was something we were used to doing when traveling or visiting friends. He sat on the toilet resting his cheek on my thigh. I played with his springy blonde curls and waited for the sound of water hitting water. When he was done, I pulled up his pajama bottoms and put him back into bed. Then, without sound or warning, from the top of his head, moving slowly down his face, he turned grey-blue. It wasn't a color I'd ever seen on him or anyone before. It terrified me. I knew it was bad. I could feel my heart thumping in my chest.

"Noah! What's the matter? What's wrong? Noah!"

I shook him, pulled him upright in the hospital bed and ran into the hall yelling for help.

Back in the room, he was grey-blue from his head to his hands now. He was dying. "No! Noah. You can't die. No. Stop. Stay with me. I need you. Come on Noah."

I ran back into the hall. "He's dying, come on. Hurry! Please help me. Please someone! Now!"

I put my mouth over his and gave him some oxygen. I did it another time, just to be sure. He continued to become more pale and blue.

"Noah, please. Come back."

Nurses ran into the room. I heard Ernestine, the hospital operator, call "Code Blue" to room 410. She repeated the message. I was ushered into the hall. I stood watching as a crash cart and the code team ran toward me and went into Noah's room.

I knew everyone on the team. I grabbed Leon, a perfusionist and part of the code team, before he ducked into the room. "Noah is in there. Help him. He's dying."

"I'll do my best," he said.

Carol, a hospital social worker, escorted me to a waiting area.

"I want to wait by his room."

"No, it's better if you're down here," she said. "I'll keep you posted about everything that happens. Do you want me to call anyone?"

"Noah's dad."

I couldn't remember his number. My mind, my thoughts and my memory were all in the room with Noah. I told her where he worked.

"I'll find him," she said.

I sat alone in a spacious waiting room at the end of the hall and tried to pray. I wanted to pray. No prayers came. As I rested my elbows on my knees, I could feel my right knee shaking. I put my hand on it to make it stop. The hand could not calm the knee. I got up and walked around the room. The shaking knee made it difficult to walk. I took some deep breaths and sat down. The knee continued to shake. I pressed two hands on it. It still shook. I willed it to stop and it refused.

"I'm Father Bart, the hospital chaplain," said a familiar voice. I looked up from my shaking knee at the tall priest. I'd heard him conduct Mass at the hospital chapel. He was Nigerian and had a melodic accent I liked.

"My son is dying. Pray for him. I need him. I love him too much."

Father Bart prayed and I tried to breathe. When he concluded, he asked, "Do you want to add anything?"

"Please, dear God, don't let Noah die. Make him well. That's all I want," I said. I crossed myself and wiped my eyes on my sleeve.

Amen.

"I'll stay until your family comes," Father Bart said.

"I'm waiting for my husband. Will you see where he is? A social worker was calling him. I just don't know where he is. I need him."

My knee was still shaking of its own accord; I watched it as I waited. I needed to talk to someone. I dialed the number of my best friend at work from my hospital days. Her four-digit number came easily. "Judy. I'm on the fourth floor. Noah coded. Come up. Help me. I'm so scared. I'm all alone."

Carol returned with a phone. "Here's your husband."

"Oh Mike. Noah started to die right in front of me. I tried my best to talk him out of it, but he was turning grey and not breathing. I gave him mouth to mouth. People are in with him right now. Yes, I think he's alive. They haven't told me anything yet. I don't know what is going on," I said.

I could hear Mike take a deep and choked breath over the phone. "I'll be right there. I'm driving now."

Carol mouthed the words, *He's okay.*

"Mike, they just told me he's okay. Hurry. Come fast. We need you."

"I'm almost there," he said before we hung up.

"They're still working on Noah. They're putting him on a ventilator. One of the doctors will be in to see you in a few minutes," Carol said.

"He's still alive?" I asked.

"Yes," she said.

Judy rushed into the room, wrapping her arms around me. She was thin and wiry but held me with a powerful grip. I wept into her shoulder. "I don't want him to die. I just love him so much."

"I know, I know. He's going to be okay. Everyone is in there with him, all the really good people. They'll make sure he lives," Judy said.

"He was dying right in front of me, Judy. I had to scream for help and they called a code. I begged Noah to come back."

"He's going to be okay. I really think he is," she said.

"That's all I want in this world," I said.

"I know. I know." She spotted Mike first, gave him a quick hug and left. "I'll go call people," she said.

Mike was panicky and pale. He kept reaching under his glasses to wipe his eyes. We silently held each other for a long time saying nothing. There were no words for our fear and dread.

I told him everything I could remember about what happened that morning and how Noah nearly died.

He shook his head and turned away from me, looking out the window. "I can't think about him not being with us. I knew he was sick, but I never thought he was *this* sick."

The ER physician, who stepped into the room, interrupted our conversation. "We're transferring Noah to DeVos Children's Hospital. He's on a ventilator now. It will keep him breathing. He needs specialized care. Aero Med will be here in about fifteen minutes."

"Aero Med?"

"Yes, he's too fragile to transport by ambulance."

"Will one of us go with him?" I asked, secretly hoping it might be me.

"No, you should drive," the doctor said. The helicopter is very crowded and they don't normally allow non-patient passengers."

"Can we see him?" I asked.

In Noah's room, a ventilator tube distorted his mouth, pulling it downward. I didn't like how it looked—painful and ugly on his sweet face. He was damp and pallid. There was blood on the sheet. I rubbed his head, whispered to him and kissed his cheek.

He wasn't responsive.

"We had to work hard to keep him." It was Leon. "He's a tough kid. He's had some meds to help him with the vent," he said.

"Please thank everyone for us," I said.

He nodded.

Mike and I held Noah's hands. They were limp and warm, covered with tape and tubes. Each hand led to an IV bag, one with doubled fluids and medicine. The ventilator was pumping away and his oxygen levels were at 99. At least he was getting the air he needed.

"Time to fly," said the ER physician. "Aero Med is about to land. You need to go back into the waiting area so we can get him packed up. You'll see him before he goes."

We kissed Noah and walked back into the bright, spacious waiting room at the end of the hall where Father Bart and I had been praying alone before. It was full of people. Judy had spread the word about Noah. Roger, the hospital CEO, my former boss Mary, and a few other people I'd worked with at Mercy were there. I managed a smile. I knew Noah *did* have the best people working on him.

Roger hugged us. "He's going to be okay," Roger said. "The code team told me what they did. He's in good hands."

The waiting room's big double door clicked and opened automatically and Noah, his bed, poles and staff came through to take him down to the helipad.

We circled him. My friends were touching his face, ruffling his hair, squeezing his toes and rubbing his shoulders—everyone was laying hands on Noah. From down the hall a stranger appeared. She was short with dark hair, wearing a red sweatshirt and jeans. Her sneakers squeaked on the polished floors. She held a single balloon, which drifted behind her as she headed our way, then slowed. I didn't recognize her. Seeing the curious expression on my face she veered toward Mike with some familiarity. "I'm Noah's bus driver. I heard at school he was sick, and I wanted to bring him a balloon," she said. "Noah likes balloons."

"Join us," Roger said. "Noah is taking a helicopter ride and we were just about to pray." We all held hands as Roger prayed. He thanked God for saving Noah's life that day and for the people in the hospital who worked with Noah. He asked that Mike and I be comforted and strong and that Noah have a safe flight and a fast recovery. We all said amen and squeezed each other's hands, holding on for an extra minute. I heard the slowing foot-foot-foot sound of the helicopter.

"Time to go," the ER physician said. We kissed Noah and squeezed his arms above the IV ports. People were saying cheerful goodbyes while he slept, unaware of the fuss. I wondered if he knew he'd come so close to dying? I was certain when he awoke he'd be happy to be with us again. Despite what people say about heaven being a *better place,* there was no better place for our son than with Mike and me.

The doctor, a nurse, and a tech took Noah down the elevator. From the window a few floors above, we watched him being loaded into the helicopter. He looked so tiny on the big stretcher, swaddled in layers of blankets. Only his face was visible. "I wish Noah knew he was riding on a helicopter. He'd be thrilled. We'll tell him about it when he wakes up," Mike said.

Slowly the rotors on the blue helicopter began to spin, and within a minute, it rose over the still bare trees into the blue spring sky and Noah flew off to the east.

❖

It was as if I was seeing my son for the first time, although I'd bathed and dressed him nearly every day of his life. He was sleeping with a ventilator tube stuck in his mouth and down his throat. IVs were pumping antibiotics, sedatives and fluids into his sixty-pound frame. He lay in the pediatric intensive care unit bed at the children's hospital wearing only underwear, and I could see each of his individual ribs. His collarbone and shoulders, where there is little muscle, were even more defined. The elastic band of the briefs lay over his hipbones and there was a pocket of space where his stomach and abdomen sunk well below his hips. His legs were long and thin and his knee bones were almost as thick as his thighs.

I was used to his skinniness. But now, as other people examined him in a nearly naked state, I was ashamed. Did they think we had starved him? He looked emaciated, wasted. I wanted to cover him up with the white flannel blanket stuffed down at the end of the bed. How was it that I didn't take in, fully see, his skeletal frame before this moment? I rubbed his head and leaned down and kissed his pale cheek, lingering close to his face.

"Is he going to be okay?" Mike asked. His hands gripped the rails of the bed.

"Yes," said the physician, "He'll need to be on the vent for a day or two, then we'll wean him off it. We need to get his lungs cleared up. They're pretty full right now."

"He almost died in front of me this morning," I said.

No one responded. The doctor was listening to his lungs with a stethoscope.

"Things are sounding better in there, even better than when he came in," he said without looking up.

"Where has Noah been?" asked the nurse who was riffling through some papers.

The question confused me. "What do you mean?"

"Well, with kids like Noah we usually see them a few times a year—some more often. Where has he been getting his care? Did you just move here?" She looked at the chart. "He's sixteen, right?"

"Yes, he's sixteen. But he's never been sick before," I said, truthfully. "I mean he's had a couple of colds and scoliosis surgery at the University of Michigan, but he's never, ever been sick like this," I said. The only medical care we had gotten for Noah had been because of his cerebral palsy and the complications from it. Physiatrists, neurologists, orthopods, and once an endocrinologist—these weren't doctors for sick kids. We were at specialist or subspecialist appointments at least six times a year, but they focused on his disability and the complications from that.

Less than a week before the Aero Med helicopter ride he'd never been admitted to our local hospital, much less this bigger, specialty children's hospital. He was a healthy disabled kid.

She looked at me skeptically. "Most kids like Noah are frequent fliers, in and out during the year with all sorts of issues. It's pretty unusual for us not have seen him before now," she said.

"Really?" I wasn't aware that kids with CP were sicklier than other kids. Noah wasn't. He'd see his pediatrician for an annual physical or for a referral if needed, but he didn't get there more than once or twice a year. "I think he's only had antibiotics maybe five times in his life. He doesn't get sick. Or didn't get sick until now," I said.

She charted his weight in the bed, which was outfitted with a scale.

"Have you ever considered a feeding tube?" the nurse said as we observed Noah in the big bed. She was touching his ribs and bony knees.

This again. The feeding tube. I thought with a sigh.

"Noah really loves to eat."

"He's a great eater," said Mike. "He loves to eat… never misses a meal."

"He can still eat food. The feeding tube would just supplement his regular meals, give him a few extra hundred calories a day. It could just run at night."

"Really?" I said. This was news to us. I wondered why no one had ever mentioned this detail before. I traced Noah's shoulder with my fingers.

❖

A year before this hospital admission, we were concerned that puberty was not coming or was coming too slowly. Noah was fifteen years old but looked like he was eleven. We secured a referral to see an endocrinologist. The doctor was a very dark man with a jovial bedside nature and a cheerful accent. Materials provided told us that he was from Ghana, West Africa. In the exam room he brought out a string of blue beads that reminded me of those that a child might put together when learning manual dexterity and pincer gripping. The beads ranged from about thumb size to walnut size. He held out the beads. "How old is he? Ah, fifteen years. This bead should be the size of his testes," he said as he chose a bead nearly at the end of the string. "Pull down your underwear," he said to Noah.

We helped him stand on the footplates of his wheelchair and pulled down the boxers he was wearing.

"See, he is only a year smaller than he should be," the doctor said as he compared the beads and the Noah's testes. Noah blushed. Mike and I laughed nervously.

"Puberty will come soon," he said.

The endocrinologist's nurse who was in the room for the examination showed us a height and weight chart she'd made some marks on. While Noah's height was somewhat close to normal, his weight was far down the curve, maybe where an eight-year-old would be. This wasn't a surprise because he'd been underweight all of his life.

"Have you considered a feeding tube? It would help Noah with his weight and the onset of puberty," she said pointing out the plots on the chart.

"No, that's not for us," I said. "We just need to work on finding more calorie dense food for him."

She didn't press us on the issue. "Let me get some nutritional brochures for you," she said.

"Noah really loves to eat," Mike said after she left the room. "He'd hate that tube."

"Sounds awful," I said.

"I'm hungry," Noah murmured.

"We'll get something on the way home, before dinner. Maybe some French fries and a burger?" Normally, we didn't feed Noah fast food, but it appeared that America's obesity problem was not Noah's problem.

The nurse gave us some information and ideas to help boost his caloric intake. We looked it over and promised to give it a shot.

He didn't gain much weight despite changes, like cooking eggs in butter instead of cooking spray. We switched him from a nutritious homemade school lunch to a calorie-laden, fat-packed school lunch. We added cheese or butter to everything we could. He didn't like ice cream or milkshakes, "It's too cold," he said. We fed him potato chips, Cheetos, regular in-between meal McDonald's double cheeseburgers, fish sandwiches, French fries and peanut M&Ms. It felt wrong to be stuffing him with unhealthy fattening foods, but we knew it was what he needed to get healthy.

❖

In the PICU, Noah was making good progress, and as promised the ventilator was dialed down and removed a day after his admission. Noah was safe, and his recovery was progressing to the physician's satisfaction. We tried to cheer Noah up with stories about his helicopter ride and encouraged him to eat, drink and breathe deeply. It was late May. He was missing the last weeks of school, and we were anxious about him being well enough to go to Bay Cliff camp in mid-June.

Now, as I looked at him in the hospital bed I knew everything we'd done to get him to gain weight hadn't worked. If only we'd known that the tube feedings would have been in addition to family meals, maybe we wouldn't be in the PICU now. I was overcome with guilt at my own stubbornness and ignorance.

"So what about a feeding tube?" asked the PICU nurse, following up with us. "Have you given it any more thought?"

"We've been talking about it and think it might be a good thing for him," said Mike. "You're sure he can still eat with us? What will it look like?"

"Of course he can eat with you. This is just for supplemental feeding, mostly at night. You won't even be able to see the tube. It will be under his shirt, and just a small button will show through the skin. Most kids do really well with it," she said, showing us illustrations in a brochure. Though we weren't fully sure of the implications, we agreed, knowing that something had to change to improve his health—and from what we'd been told, his weight was at the heart of it.

Just ten days after his admission, when he'd gained enough lung capacity and strength to endure the short surgery, a feeding tube was inserted and, as the nurse promised, it wasn't as invasive as we'd thought it might be. When Noah was successfully taking food through the tube, we all went home and tried to remember where we'd left off. It was summer now, Memorial Day weekend had passed, school was over for the year—three weeks had gone by since his helicopter ride.

In retrospect, I think the delay in the feeding tube insertion had to do with who we were: middle class, white, married, professional people. We showed up at appointments on time, were prepared for procedures, knew Noah's history, paid our bills, brought the paperwork we were asked to bring, asked questions—but not too many—and when we said no, no one ever questioned us or pushed us. When we declined the feeding tube the first time, medical professionals must have assumed our thoughts were well reasoned and our income, perhaps, kept us off the radar screen of social workers. Our fault? Maybe. Despite our education, we didn't know everything, and I believe in some ways we slipped through the cracks of the system. Noah should have had a feeding tube several years before we agreed to it. I sometimes wonder if extra weight might have prolonged his life. This haunts me, even makes me angry, especially when I see young people with CP around Noah's age who appear to be thriving. I should have known that when I never saw anyone, not even in pictures, as thin as Noah, that something was very wrong.

❖

The feeding tube really wasn't a tube at all, not externally anyway. It was unobtrusive, like a dime-sized Tupperware lid. It sat flat on his belly a few inches above his navel. When we hooked it up to the pumping machine, we gave it a little twist and the tube locked in. When he was done feeding, we'd snap on a cap. His stomach fluids didn't leak out, which surprised me. I was sure it would be messier than it really was. The bag of Ensure (two cans a night, vanilla) went from an IV-like pump right into Noah's stomach connected to several feet of tubing and to a feedbag (as we called it) hung high on a pole. The parts all fit neatly together and snapped into place like a construction set. The pump was metered for eight hours, quietly moving food into Noah's gut as he slept. The pump made a very quiet whirring sound and an occasional soft click. It had a beeping alarm, and if the bag emptied, it had to be shut off.

One morning at about 3:30, the pump's alarm sounded. We slept through it, but Noah woke up. "Mom! Come here, Mom!" he called.

I dashed down the spiral staircase to his room. "I'm all wet," Noah said. The tube had come un-hitched and he was lying in a puddle of sticky, vanilla scented, yellow, vitamin-tinged Ensure. "I'm cold," he said.

"Mike! I need some help. We have a mess down here."

Noah's lambskin mattress pad, flannel sheets and his mattress protector all needed to go into the washing machine, and Noah into the shower. I carried everything carefully so it wouldn't drip on the carpet. We ran the washer and shower and mopped up the mattress, which had a dinner plate-sized sticky spot. We made a pot of coffee. There was no point in going back to sleep.

In spite of the mishap, I came to love the feedbag. It was handy for putting additives into Noah's Ensure. I could toss in a scoop of body builder grade protein powder and up the calories and nutritional value. I could mix in crushed up vitamins that he otherwise would never eat and help keep him healthy. With a comically large syringe, I could shoot medications that normally made him gag or puke through the tube and into his belly. When he had a sniffle, I crushed up a garlic clove, sent it in through the tube, easing his symptoms without the bad breath. Life was easier with the feeding tube, and he was gaining weight. Not a lot, but in three weeks he was up two pounds.

His pediatrician was pleased with his progress during a follow-up visit. "I don't think Noah will ever be heavy, and that's probably a good thing. But his gains so far look good," he said.

"Can he go to camp this summer?" I asked.

"I want to go to Bay Cliff," Noah chimed in. "I feel good. I can breathe," he added, selling his pediatrician on his good health.

We discussed the start date and determined that he could go two weeks after the camp's official opening day. I'd called the camp and was assured that the nursing staff and counselors had worked with feeding tubes before, so it wouldn't be a problem for them.

His pediatrician left the room for what seemed like a long time. When he returned, he paused and thought. He looked at his notes and then spoke. "The student nurse, the one who was just in here, she's working in the nursing unit at Bay Cliff this summer. She'll keep an eye on him and will call in Noah's weight and breathing progress to me each week," he said.

"I'm going to camp! I can't wait," Noah said. His face was lit by his smile; I had not seen him this happy in many weeks.

I felt a lump form in my throat. His brush with death a month ago seemed like it was setting a course for the rest of his life. All I could envision was a life of precautions and caution—more doctors' and specialist visits, more durable medical equipment and a feeding tube. Going to camp was more normal, and normal was all we wanted.

CHAPTER 15 | Bay Cliff

Noah and friends at camp.

We were standing on the shore of Lake Superior at Pictured Rocks near Munising on a clear and warm summer morning; the sun reflected on the giant wet rocks in a vivid striped pinkish-khaki. Mike and I were taking advantage of a week away from work and being parents while Noah was at Indian Trails Camp, outside of Grand Rapids. It is curious to think that the chance encounter about to occur would shape our son's life. There were ten of us in the group and everyone was wearing precautionary wetsuits, as the water temperature was around 45 degrees. Everyone in the group seemed to know each other, except Mike and me. Mike introduced us.

"My name is Mike, and this is my wife, Roberta. We're from Muskegon and we have a son with some disabilities. We're always looking for boats we can get him into, so we thought we'd check out kayaking," he said.

"I'm Nancy," a tall, tan and slender woman began. "I'm an adaptive paddling instructor at Bay Cliff. Everyone here is from the camp. Today is our day off. Bay Cliff is a camp near Marquette for kids with disabilities like your son."

We perked up like dogs who'd just heard the words "treats" or "car ride." We were always on the lookout for programs that might help Noah.

While we paddled over giant green rocks that lie below the brilliant and clear Lake Superior waters and close to the colorful Pictured Rocks, we quizzed the staff. They were physical and occupational therapists, mostly school-based during the year and working at the camp for the summer. Their enthusiasm for the camp and its programs sold us on a visit. Nancy scribbled the camp director's name and phone number on a business card for us. We called right after the kayak trip and asked for an appointment to see him and the camp.

Mr. Tim was a serious man. Maybe he just seemed that way because we called and stopped by the camp mid-session, or perhaps it was that we were from downstate. Bay Cliff is an Upper Peninsula (U.P.) thing, and they treated people from below the Mackinac Bridge with reticence.

"So do you have any kids here from the Lower Peninsula?" I asked.

He paused. "Yes, this year we had space for three campers from downstate," he said. "But kids from the U.P. are our priority. When we have all of our U.P. kids placed, then we look at applicants from downstate."

"Makes sense," I said, but not really following or believing the logic of differentiation. Admittedly, Michigan has an odd geography. The northern part of the state is physically hooked onto Wisconsin and the Lower Peninsula connects to the U.P. only by a bridge built in 1956. The distinction between the two parts seemed unfair, but it wasn't time to debate. I wanted my son to go to camp at Bay Cliff.

"You can apply next summer and if we have space," he said, "we'll consider taking Noah. He must be able to benefit from the therapies we offer. We work very closely with school therapists and teachers. We need to make sure the goals our campers are working on in school are what we can accomplish here."

This sounded just like what Noah needed, intensive daily physical, occupational and speech therapies. Summer was such a gap of time for his progress. With school out and insurance not covering ongoing therapy, Noah tended to lose the skills he'd built during the school year.

We also needed a break. The closeness of our family could be overwhelming. Other than this trip up north, a week at another camp the prior summer and a few overnights when we persuaded friends and relatives to take Noah, we were rarely separated from him. Caregivers, even the most loving parents, need a break. Bay Cliff was more than we expected for a break.

"Camp is eight weeks long. You know that, right?" said Mr. Tim.

"Yes. It seems like a long time."

"It is, but for the therapy to be effective and for the children to meet their goals, we need that much time," he explained.

Leaving Noah for this long was hard to imagine.

"Where is Noah now?" asked Mr. Tim.

I mentioned Indian Trails.

"Ah yes, a good recreational camp," he said. He emphasized *recreation*. "I know the director there." He looked at his watch. "Would you like to join us for lunch?"

Mike and I hesitated.

"The food is very good, home cooked, nutritious and fresh. For some of our kids, it is the best food they eat all year," he said. "You'll be able to meet some of the campers and staff."

Lunch was held in the Big House, aptly named because it was the biggest building on the Camp's property. The Big House was noisy, filled with kids laughing and talking, manual wheelchairs, power chairs, walkers, white canes for the visually impaired and even a service dog to add to the congestion. A long ramp led campers and staff in, and the windows were screened all around, perfect for hot summer days and keeping out the U.P.'s biting black flies.

One of the campers led the group in grace and Mr. Tim introduced Mike and me as special guests and asked us to stand. The kids applauded to welcome us. I tried to smile, but my jaw was tight and my lower lip was pulled in. I wanted so badly to see Noah in this scene, in this place, that I was crying.

"These are his people," I said to Mike. Bay Cliff was a big community of people with disabilities, and I knew that we, as able-bodied people, couldn't provide this kind of peer environment for Noah. The campers were independent and strong. They were moving so fast in their wheelchairs, cutting closely around the other kids and the tables. It all seemed so normal.

"I wish Noah could see this," Mike said. "I think he'd like it here."

❖

The camp is a former dairy farm, but as long as it has been a camp it has served kids in need. Two women, a public health physician and a nurse, who traveled the U.P. helping malnourished and underweight children and their families, founded it. The Great Depression took its toll on the mining families in the region with grinding poverty and illness. The women dreamed of a place where they could bring the children for the summer, give them good food, sunshine and exercise.

Despite the Depression, they were able to find others who believed in their dream and the 170-acre dairy farm in Big Bay was purchased and became Bay Cliff Health Camp. In 1934, just over one hundred underweight kids were brought to the camp, and on average each gained five pounds over the summer. The camp adapted to the times and when the Depression ended, Polio struck the country and the U.P., the women began to work with children affected by Polio. The camp provided patient care and physical therapy—thus setting in place what it would become known for—serving children with physical disabilities.

❖

Noah was thirteen years old the first summer we took him to Bay Cliff. As Mr. Tim promised, the application process was rigorous. The packet arrived and there were papers for Mike and me to complete. There were forms for his occupational, physical, speech and music therapists to complete and return, too. His teacher, principal and physician also had to account for Noah's physical, mental and moral fitness to attend camp.

"This must be what it's like to fill out college application papers," I said to Mike. After the papers were completed and returned, we waited. Bay Cliff was reviewing all applications and downstate and out-of-state kids would be notified in mid-May. Mid-May came and I couldn't stand it any longer. I called Miss Karen, the educational director, whom I had also called earlier to make sure Noah's paperwork was complete. I wasn't going to let him miss out on camp due to a technical issue.

"Let's see. I was just finishing my staffing. Noah… Noah… Ah! Here he is," she paused.

I held my breath.

"Yes, we have space for him this summer."

"Oh yes! Thank you. Thank you so much. This means everything to me. To Noah. Thank you!" I said. She told me the official acceptance letter would be in the mail soon.

"Noah, you're in at Bay Cliff!" I announced when he came home from school.

He'd heard his dad and me talking about the camp all winter long.

All he said was, "That's good."

❖

Noah steered his powerchair right toward us.

"Wow. Look at him, Mike," I said.

"He really seems to get it. Practically going in a straight line," he said.

We walked in his direction—I might have even run a bit. It seemed like a very long time since we dropped him off at camp.

"Noah! How are you? Oh I missed you so much." I kissed and hugged him. He looked different. He seemed older and more confident.

"Can I come back next year?" he asked.

I was almost speechless. Where was *Mom, I missed you and Dad so much* or *I'm so happy to see you.* He'd separated from us so cleanly.

"Well, can I?" he asked again.

"It was that much fun?"

"I love Bay Cliff," he said.

"Then, I guess we'll have to work on getting you back next summer," Mike said. "What did you do all summer?"

"Therapy. Swimming in the pool. Had a parade. Ate goulash. Motorcycles came up and Indian dancers," said Noah.

He started chuckling out loud. "I told a joke," he said.

"To whom?"

"My therapy group. I told them," he said.

"Tell us," Mike said. "Noah has a joke."

"Why don't cannibals eat clowns?" Noah said, trying not to laugh and mess up the joke.

"Why?" Mike and I said in unison.

"Because they taste funny!" Noah grinned.

We laughed loud and hard. It was a big accomplishment for Noah to tell an entire joke.

❖

Just out of Marquette, past Northern Michigan University's wooden Superior Dome, there's a turn to County Road 550. That's where I'd move to the back seat of the van to sit next to Noah and hold his hand. Mike would drive, and we'd put on a Jimmy Buffett CD and try to make the mood lighter. Noah loved going to camp, and we knew that taking him there would be the highlight of his year, something we'd talk about for months. But dropping him off and saying goodbye for eight weeks was never easy. We missed his presence and the time we weren't spending on his care was sometimes hard to fill. His time at camp was a bittersweet time for us alone without him.

I tried not to get too emotional as we wound up the road past Phil's 550 Store, cottages, homes and the occasional rustic resort cabin complex.

"You're going to have so much fun this summer, Noah. Wonder if any of your old cabin mates will be back?" I said, cheerfully.

"I don't know. Maybe," said Noah.

"You'll be in the same cabin this year—Sam's. That's good," I said.

"Guess so," Noah said as he looked out the window. He was very stoic during this ride up to camp.

I squeezed his hand. "I'll write to you every single day," I promised. I'd already mailed a few postcards before we left so he'd get one on the first day of camp.

"Thanks, Mom."

Noah's changes after a summer were obvious to Mike and me. Simply, he came back better than when we sent him. He spoke in sentences that were more complete and louder. He was better at articulating his observations. He was more willing and able to feed himself. He was a better wheelchair driver. Stronger. At least a few pounds heavier. What Bay Cliff did for him, at its essence, was immerse him in a community of people with all sorts of disabilities and encourage him to have a voice.

The 456 miles from Muskegon to Big Bay and eight weeks away was what Noah needed to help him mature from our little boy to an independent teen. His five summers spent up over the Mackinac Bridge helped distance him from parents who would do anything and everything for him, and helped him realize he was as much abled as disabled.

After Death Stories

When you are sorrowful look again in your heart,
and you shall see that in truth, you are weeping
for that which has been your delight.
—Kahlil Gibran

chapter 16 | Homeward Bound

Dashboard cherub.

Through the darkness, in our own personal solitude, the three of us rode home from the hospital Noah-less. I made phone calls to friends while Mike drove. As miles passed on the snowy expressway, I reviewed the saved numbers in my phone, wondering who needed to know and who could hear the news in the morning. Tasha sat in the backseat of the MINI silently. Even when we passed McDonald's she didn't ask to stop.

Home wasn't the old yellow house we bought from Dan, but another place that Mike designed and built ten years before. To accommodate Noah's wheelchair, ramps led to both the front and back doors and it had an airy, open floor plan. Noah had been able to travel easily throughout our house.

Mail and newspapers were piled on the kitchen table and the house smelled stale and unlived in, like we'd been on vacation. We'd been missing for two weeks. Suddenly, it didn't feel much like home at all. I helped Tasha get ready for bed and sat with her as she cried and quizzed me about the evening's events.

"But, why did he die?"

"I don't know. I wish I had an explanation for you, honey."

"I'm about to be missing him, Mom. I want to be with him."

"Me, too. Try to relax and sleep. You don't have to go to school tomorrow. Sleep in if you want," I said as I rubbed her back and dried her tears.

Later, I sat at my desk trying to compose Noah's obituary while Mike and Tasha slept. Grief conflicted with my thoughts about Noah's life, who he was as a human and how I, as the writer and his mother, would portray him. There were so many details I wanted to include: his high school academic letter and varsity jacket, pulling the school fire alarm in the sixth grade, his solid Catholic faith and summers at Bay Cliff Health Camp. I'd write a few sentences and stop because I was thinking too hard about him. I wandered downstairs to Noah's room, looking around for inspiration or to make sure I didn't miss anything. My heart ached being in his room late at night and seeing his bed flat and empty, knowing it would be that way from now on.

I looked at the books I'd read him as a baby: *The Mitten* and *Chicken Soup with Rice* were favorites. I paged through *Curious George Makes Pancakes*, *Charlotte's Web* and *The BFG*, looking for the parts we both enjoyed. I looked at the first Harry Potter book and remembered reading it to him. I opened his dresser and riffled through his clothes. A pair of plaid flannel pants I loved seeing Noah wear caught my eye and I felt lightheaded and thought I might faint. I sat on the edge of his bed and breathed deeply; then I lay down there amongst his pillows and stuffed animals and cried hard.

Few parents can imagine what it means to write your own child's obituary. Each word and idea matters more than any other word ever written. My throat tightened and my chest ached. My eyes burned as I searched for the right words and tone, the perfect sequence of life events and personality traits that made Noah, Noah. As I wrote, I smiled and ached. For a moment I would be immersed in a memory and a place I loved, only to return to the work. Reading it aloud was even more difficult than writing. My voice was rough and I stopped over and over to cry and revise. Just before dawn, I completed the obituary. Then I went to bed and fell asleep praying and hoping that Noah would visit me in my dreams.

CHAPTER 17 | What I Wrote

Noah's obituary photo, taken at his Confirmation.

Miesch, Noah William
Muskegon

Noah Miesch died on February 27, 2006, in the presence of his adoring parents Mike Miesch and Roberta King, who kissed and hugged on him until he took his last breath and made his way to heaven.

Noah was born on September 23, 1988, and was proud to be a Big Red and a sophomore at Muskegon High School. He also had attended Bluffton, Marquette and Bunker schools. His school years were noted by his achievement of a freshman academic letter that he proudly wore on his varsity jacket and for testing the fire alarm at Marquette Elementary, which earned him a three-day suspension. Noah was an amazing kid who lived a full and happy life. He was generous with his smiles and was known for his great sense of humor and his ability to engage and test people. Noah lived and loved life and thoroughly cared about the people in his world. He enjoyed spending summers at Bay Cliff Health Camp in Big Bay; taking spring break trips to the Florida Keys and swimming with the dolphins; boating and going to happy hour in Key West. He loved Jimmy Buffett concerts; SpongeBob SquarePants cartoons; hanging out with Bob and Dick; swimming in the Harbor Towne Yacht Club pool or having Friday dinner there; soaking in the hot tub at home; going to Mass at Our Lady of Grace; Christmas; snow tubing and sledding and the many meals he shared with family, friends and neighbors.

He leaves behind his parents, his sister Tasha Miesch, his grandfather Bob King, great-uncle Dick King; his grandmother Ann Miesch and aunts and uncles Jan and Al, Chuck and Kathy,

Bob and Shelly and Bill and Linda; his Lutheran Godparents Gary and Laura Yelsik of Saginaw; his Catholic Godparents Jane Clingman Scott and Greg Scott; and special friends Joy Hamilton of Shelby and Phil Chmura. Memorial contributions should be made to Bay Cliff Health Camp or to the Community Foundation for Muskegon County.

CHAPTER 18 | Bravest Person in the Room

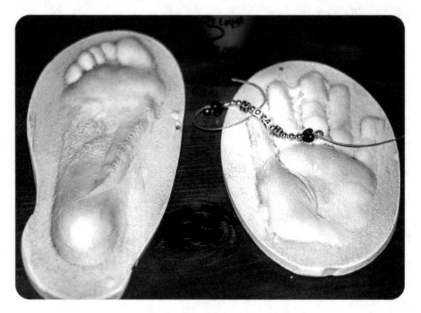

Noah's hand and foot casted at DeVos Children's Hospital.

"I 'll be right there," Jane said when I called. I needed her. I needed someone to be my navigator and Jane stepped in because she knew what to do. Her own daughter had died at the age of seventeen, too.

The morning after Noah's death, Jane came to our house with *Gather,* the Catholic hymnal. She helped us choose scripture readings for the funeral and the hymns the choir and mourners would sing. As a lifelong Catholic, she knew what would work and the best choices for a child's funeral rather than what might be in an adult service. We let her lead us, her own experience giving her the aura of solemnity we needed. She came with Mike and me to meet with Father Mike at the church to plan the funeral.

A day or so before Noah's visitation I was telling a friend how anxious I was, and he told me, "You'll be the calmest person there." I didn't believe it at the time, but it was true. At the visitation, people were more outwardly grieving, more upset than Mike and I. Yes, we cried with people, we hugged, we listened to them try to express feelings and express their anxiety about not knowing what to say. People are uncomfortable with the death of a child. We have a litany of reasons when older people die. He had a good life. She was old and the time was right. She was suffering and ready to go. But kids? Never. Kids should never die. I felt like I had to be calm and brave for other people. I knew I needed to help them get through their discomfort and grief, so I could get through mine.

The visitation room at the funeral home had the thickest carpet I'd ever stood on; it was like standing on a wrestling mat. If I were to faint, no harm would have come to my head. There was music in the background, but nothing I could identify—it wasn't classical or popular music. I asked Dan if there were other choices. "Do you have anything more... interesting? Maybe more cheerful?" They didn't, and there was no need as soon the voices of people overwhelmed the room.

I wore a black skirt and sweater for the visitation, and comfortable black pumps. I figured I wouldn't get a chance to sit for over three hours. Mike wore a sport coat and a tie. We had a hard time finding an appropriate tie because most of his ties were artful, wild or colorful. "I guess this one will do," he said, choosing one that was green and purple. He wore the only good shoes he owned, a pair of dark green Doc Marten wingtips. Tasha dressed in jeans and a new dark blue sweater that we bought the afternoon before the visitation.

We had to make a trip to the mall that afternoon for funeral clothing. *A funeral suit*, I thought. *I'm buying special clothes for my son's funeral.* I settled on a black suit with tiny green flecks in the material. After the funeral, I had a tailor shorten the skirt and I wore it to work a few times before giving it to Goodwill. It was always Noah's funeral suit, and I couldn't wear it without remembering why I bought it.

Tasha was enjoying the company of all the kids who showed up at the visitation. She and Noah had many of the same friends. Every once in a bit I'd see her holding someone's hand and taking them up to the spot where the box of ashes was sitting.

All of our neighbors from our tiny channel-side street stopped at the visitation—together. They must have planned it when they were making arrangements to drop off meals for us. They were mostly people our age, some younger, but they all had kids of their own. These were normally talkative and outgoing people, and now they were having trouble expressing themselves. I could practically read what they were thinking on their faces, "This could be my child."

After Noah's visitation, we were milling around the funeral home and Jane told us we needed to go get some dinner. I was surprised. It seemed strange to me that we'd do such a thing. I thought we would go straight home, shut off the lights and go to sleep. It was already 9:00 p.m. The visitation ran over by almost an hour. We all went over to Mangos, a nearby restaurant for drinks, dinner and decompression from the visitation. It was a good decision; we talked about who was there (a few hundred people by the guest book) and the things people had to say about Noah.

"One of his speech therapists told me something funny," I said. "I guess the guy had a really tiny office and Noah would be in there for therapy and would fart and say 'Phew! You stink,' to the therapist, passing the blame. He and the therapist would go back and forth teasing about who actually tooted."

"Cindy told me a great story about Noah," Mike said. "One day at daycare when she was getting him up off the toilet and went to pull up his pants, she lost her balance. She and Noah fell into the empty bathtub with Noah's pants still around his ankles. He was on top of her and she couldn't get out. Cindy had to call for help to rescue them. Noah was just laughing and laughing."

We laughed a lot that evening, something I would never have guessed was possible at that time.

❖

Ten years before Noah's death, Jane's daughter Brigid's visitation had been packed with young people. She was a junior at Muskegon Catholic Central and previously attended Muskegon High, so the funeral home was jammed with groups of teens from both schools. Private school kids in one cluster, public school kids in another. Pods of girls with running mascara and clenched tissues; boys trying to comfort crying girlfriends; and groups of single boys standing with hands jammed in scruffy jeans pockets scanning the room looking for someone to extricate them from this new and odd situation. When someone in a high school dies, everyone who knows him or her or knows someone who knows him or her *must* be present. It is an event. Without filter or reservation, Brigid's friends hugged and held one another, cried loudly and comforted each other, often with long, group embraces.

Brigid had long, wavy brilliant red hair and pale, almost translucent skin with a sprinkle of freckles across a perfectly pointed nose. She was slender, almost waif-like. As I looked at her in the casket, I remembered her light blue-green eyes. "She looks like an Irish princess," I whispered to Mike.

Brigid took her own life when she was just seventeen years old.

Her suicide came after numerous hospitalizations, years of psychiatry and psychology, and continuous, diligent efforts to help her with her bipolar disorder by her parents, Jane and Greg, along with teachers and friends.

In the center of the teen grief at Brigid's visitation was a calm, or seemingly calm, Jane. Amidst of all these teens and her own friends, she stood brave and stoic—hugging, comforting, talking and even smiling.

"How could this be?" I'd thought at the time. "I'd be a mess." I imagined myself as Jane: I was sure that I would have been swallowed up in a big funeral home chair unable to stand, talk or think. I hugged Jane, and I was crying hard as I expressed my disbelief and sadness that Brigid was gone. My mother had died just a few weeks before, also suddenly, and perhaps it was an extension of that raw grief, but I clearly recall being almost crippled at Brigid's visitation. I kept thinking about Noah, who was just six years old and at home with my dad that evening. A random thought about Noah's mortality came to me. I quickly sent it away. Thoughts about our children dying are thoughts no parent ever wants to have, but I know every parent who reads a child's obituary or attends a child's funeral has the wicked, horrid thought about the death of a child they love.

I kept glancing over at Brigid's casket. I couldn't help myself.

❖

As I think back to the time of Brigid's death, I now know why Jane seemed so brave and calm. The day of Noah's visitation I found myself fearless, the bravest person in the room. I wasn't sure until now where that strength came from. Were prayers being answered? Was it adrenaline? I don't think the strength came from within me. It came from the people in the room and from the outpouring of love for Noah. People telling me their stories of how he meant something to them buoyed me. Their honest and loving tributes made me brave, and Noah made me proud.

Since Noah's funeral, more often than I expect, I have met parents who have had a child die. Sometimes they're adult children and sometimes they're kids. From a box of special notecards I keep, I write a handwritten note telling them they're in my thoughts and that I know the kind of sorrow they're feeling. It is a difficult note to write because I'm never sure if what matters to me also matters to them. I usually rip up two or three cards before I land on the right message. I think it is important that they know someone else understands what they're experiencing and has walked the same uncharted and frightening path. All bereaved parents face what I've faced—that many people are uncomfortable with the reality of children dying and aren't even sure what to say or how to express sympathy, so they avoid saying anything at all. This is painful. We wonder if people don't know or just don't care. Parents love talking about their kids, living or not. Even if it makes us grieve again, we are always grateful for the opportunity to remember their lives and share their stories.

chapter 19 | Noah's Funeral

Bedroom shelf.

Preface

There is so much about Noah's death I remember, but the actual funeral Mass is fuzzy. I feel like my memory has been coated with Vaseline. I can see the church, with Noah's box of ashes at the front with colorful flowers surrounding him. There's a choir of church members who are moving around the front, adjusting chairs and testing the sound system. In my mind, I see Father Mike checking the altar and arranging things. But I can't remember the actual funeral in the sharp way I wish I could. I think it might be because there were so many people there, not only the people I expected to see, but others who had come from across the state or left work early to be with us. I was surprised and honored by who was in the church that afternoon. All of my co-workers were there—the president had closed the Community Foundation where I worked for the funeral. Foundation trustees were there, too. I stood in the aisle for a bit watching people come in, talking with them and hugging. Hugging a lot. When there's nothing to say, a hug fills the empty and blank spaces.

Planning

There had been a bit of hurry-up and wait for Noah's funeral. He died on a Monday afternoon just before Lent. The next day was Fat Tuesday, then Ash Wednesday. We could have had the service on a Thursday, I suppose. But at this point, it seemed like Friday would work best. "Breaks up the week less," I said to Father Mike as we met in the church office one evening to finalize the plans. "Maybe a little later in the day, in case people have to work." I wasn't in a hurry, either. The holding pattern gave me time to think, plan and attempt to control my emotions.

We settled on three o'clock. "So you won't need a lunch," said the secretary at the funeral meeting at the church one afternoon.

"Umm. No. Are we supposed to? Do we have to? Did I pick the wrong time?" I asked

Jane quickly interjected, "We'll have something at my house afterward."

"Your hair smells like dye," said Tasha randomly, in front of the priest, parish secretary, Jane and Mike.

"Maybe that's because I got my hair dyed today," I said in an unkind voice, badly wanting to add in something profane to the end of the sentence. I gave her *the look* instead and she stopped talking.

We chose two hymns to sing, "Surely the Presence of the Lord is in this Place" and "On Eagle's Wings." I wanted to hear the "Ave Maria" sung, too. We needed to find people in Noah's life for the various roles in a Catholic funeral mass—readers and gift bearers. Mike wanted his co-worker Karl to read the gospel and Kitty, Noah's school aide, his teacher Julie and his Uncle Chuck would bring the communion gifts to the altar. We planned to ask Regina, Noah's friend from school to read, too.

As we discussed roles and responsibilities in the service, I drifted off. The yellow painted cinder block room seemed warm and overly bright. I really didn't know what I was doing. My mother's funeral was the only other one I'd been involved in. She had pre-planned it when she retired. She wasn't sick or anything—she just didn't want my dad and me to screw it up, although she claimed she was doing it to make it easy on us. All we did was show her plan to the pastor, give her obituary to the funeral director and make a few phone calls. Done and done.

I wanted, needed, Noah's funeral mass to be memorable, not only by what was said or the verses read and the music we would sing together, but by the intangible spirit of the ceremony. It had to reflect Noah, his life, our love for him and his relationships in our community. I wanted people to remember him (or for those who didn't know him) to learn that he lived a life that mattered and that his death would leave Mike, me, and our community forever changed.

Joy

The first time Joy sang the *Ave Maria* was for Noah's funeral. She was my best friend and had known Noah since he was a baby. We'd spent many days with her, boating, listening to live music, dancing, making elaborate meals and being family friends. She was among the first people we called when Noah got sick and after he died.

"What can I do for you?" she asked.

"I need you to sing 'Ave Maria' for Noah."

It was Tuesday afternoon and the service was Friday.

"I've never sung it, but I'd be honored, and I'll figure it out," she said. Joy bought the sheet music for the song and began practicing. She didn't know Latin and while she was vaguely familiar with the music, as a Congregationalist, she wasn't as immersed in the music as a Catholic might be. She worked with Jane and Greg who were members of the church choir and who were organizing the music for the service. Joy's friend Jim, who spent a bit of time in Catholic seminary, helped her with the Latin. Her clear soprano voice is perfect for the "Ave Maria." I had no doubt that whatever she gave it would be heavenly.

As we milled around the church before the funeral she walked in, hugged me long like she always did, but said nothing and moved quickly to the pew near the piano, a few rows up and across the aisle from Mike and me. "I couldn't talk with you," she said after the service. "If I had, I wouldn't have been able to sing. I would have just been crying." As the service progressed, she stood up, went to the microphone in front of the choir and sang the "Ave Maria" a cappella. Her voice filled the church and people were silent. She sang it perfectly from the long first note and its distinctive, *ahh*. She sang it without accompaniment because moments before the funeral began, she discovered the pianist didn't have the sheet music in the same key that Joy had learned the song.

"I just thought about being brave and strong for Noah and knew he'd help bring me through," she said.

Bob

A few weeks before Noah went into the hospital, we went to a "paint your own" ceramic studio to paint bowls for Community Kettle, a soup-themed fundraiser for Catholic Charities of West Michigan's food pantries. Noah, Tasha and I each painted a soup bowl that would be donated to the event. In addition to the donated bowl, people at the fundraiser selected a bowl to take home as a souvenir of the event—a reminder of community food insecurity. Noah painted his with a big brush, placing stripes in red, yellow and blue on the outside and painting the inside solid yellow. We set the charity bowls aside and Noah painted a star shaped bowl to take home and Tasha decorated an olive boat. We planned to attend the Community

Kettle with Bob and Sue, but when Noah became ill, I had to call and cancel. Bob was worried and asked what he could do to help. I hesitated, then asked.

"I need you to go to the event and find the bowl that Noah painted."

"I can do that. What's it look like?" he asked.

"There are two kinds of bowls, flat and wide or tall and narrow. This one is tall."

"Got it. Got it. Tall and narrow. What else?"

"Big stripes in red, blue and yellow."

"Is it signed or anything?"

"No, but the inside is a solid color. Yellow or red, I think. Maybe it's blue.

It's one of the stripe colors."

"I'll go there early and look for it."

At the event he told the volunteers he was looking for a bowl created by a kid in the hospital who was about to die. "I need to find it for his mom," he said. The volunteers gave him early access to the bowls. In all, there were five hundred bowls on a half dozen tables and Bob began sorting.

The phone in Noah's hospital room rang.

"I think I have it. Big stripes, red, blue and yellow. Yellow center."

"Yes!" I was beyond thrilled. Knowing that Noah was close to death, I wanted to keep everything of his.

"I knew you'd find it, Bob! You were the perfect person for the job."

"Roberta, if it isn't the right bowl when I bring it to you, let's just pretend it is."

"Deal." It wasn't until later when Bob told his story that I realized what a challenging task it had been: "First table, no bowl. Second table, no bowl. I'm looking through piles and stacks of bowls for a tall one with big stripes. Now, people are coming in for the event and taking their souvenir bowls. I'm watching what they're taking and looking for the bowl at the same time. I've got to find Noah's bowl. Finally I found one that I thought might be it—that I really hoped was the right one."

The bowl was, in fact, the very bowl Noah painted. I knew it the minute I saw it. I brought it to Father Mike just before the funeral, telling him how the bowl came to be and its original purpose.

"Do you think we can somehow use it in the funeral?" I asked.

"Yes, of course." He took the brightly painted bowl and went to prepare for the Mass.

When he set the communion table on the altar, the body of Christ was in Noah's bowl.

Regina

Regina went to school at Bluffton Elementary School with Noah from kindergarten to the fifth grade. Her mom, Cindy, was his daycare provider for all his elementary and most of his middle school years, so Cindy, Noah and Regina were together before and after school for a long stretch. When we met with Father Mike to plan Noah's funeral, we needed to find two people willing to read scripture. Mike asked Karl, his co-worker and close friend. I wanted a friend of Noah's to read. Regina is a devout Catholic, and we were members of the same church.

"Father Mike, would it be okay to have someone young read? I'd like one of Noah's friends to be part of the service. I was thinking of Regina."

Without hesitating he said, "Perfect. Regina will do a good job."

It was hard calling and asking. I was trying to be conscious of the effect of the death of a friend on a teen. I didn't want her to have to struggle with the reading or the decision to read at the funeral.

I called her mom first. "Yes," Cindy said, "You should ask her. I know she will want to do it."

Through tears and with a lump in my throat I asked her if she would read from Ecclesiastes 3 v. 1-8, *for everything there is a season.*

"Yes, I'd be glad to," she said.

"The funeral is at 3 o'clock on Friday. Will you be out of school?"

"I'm already planning on being there." Of course she was.

Regina was one of Noah's most mature, confident and quiet friends. She was solid, reliable and steady. In front of a church filled with friends and family she stepped up to the lectern and read. Her voice wavered and was soft at times, but it never cracked and it was beautiful.

There is a time for everything, and a season for every activity under the heavens:
a time to be born and a time to die,
a time to plant and a time to uproot,
a time to kill and a time to heal,
a time to tear down and a time to build,
a time to weep and a time to laugh,
a time to mourn and a time to dance,

a time to scatter stones and a time to gather them,
a time to embrace and a time to refrain from embracing,
a time to search and a time to give up,
a time to keep and a time to throw away,
a time to tear and a time to mend,
a time to be silent and a time to speak,
a time to love and a time to hate,
a time for war and a time for peace.

Greg

Greg volunteered to deliver Noah's eulogy and we didn't need to provide any details or additional information because he was a good storyteller and he'd spent enough time with Noah to really know him.

He recounted a snorkeling excursion to Key West our family took with Jane and him. "And just as if it happened every day, we loaded his wheelchair onto the excursion boat and when it came time to get in the water, Mike and Roberta fitted him with his snorkel and mask, took hold of him, and guided him into the ocean water."

"Noah lived a life that didn't let his disability get in his way. His parents made sure that he did the things that other kids did and sometimes more," he said.

"Another time, we all went snow tubing," he said describing us dragging Noah's wheelchair across the packed snow to a rope lift on the hill. "His dad put him in one tube, took another tube and down the hill they went. Of course, Noah flew out of his tube, got snow up his jacket and in his face, and lost a boot somewhere on the hill."

It's possible I don't remember all of Greg's stories because he described our day-to-day life with Noah. The stories he recounted were ordinary to us, but I was pleased to know that they seemed extraordinary to another person. I hoped as Noah lived, it felt that way to him too.

Leaving

Bob Dylan wrote the song "Forever Young" in 1973. I was most familiar with the cover by Rod Stewart that was popular in 1988, the year Noah was born. Stewart's expanded version included lyrics that were more tender, poetic and prophetic than Dylan's. I loved hearing Stewart's lyrics when Noah was a newborn, and now seventeen years later the words seemed perfect for someone who died too young, like Noah. The sentiments seemed to be all a parent could ask for. "Forever Young" played when people left the church from Noah's funeral.

In my heart you'll always remain, forever young.

For me, this is one of the greatest realities of Noah's death: in my heart and mind Noah will always remain forever young. I can't imagine what he would be like now at age twenty-three or any age beyond seventeen.

May the good Lord be with you
Down every road you roam

My greatest wishes for my son are that he is in companionship with the Lord and that he is in a safe and warm place. I'll never subscribe to the idea that heaven is a better place, as in *He's in a better place now.* The best place for Noah was at home with his dad and me. A child belongs with his parents, not in a far-off place, no matter how celestial and perfect it is.

May your guiding light be strong
Build a stairway to Heaven
With a prince or a vagabond
Be courageous and be brave,
And in my heart you'll always stay
Forever young

As we sent Noah off into an unknown place, I saw bravery and courage on his face. He was braver than we were at that moment. From his passing, I've learned to be fearless and to stand up for what is right and just. When I need courage or strength, I just close my eyes, imagine him as he passed from life to death, and I feel the strength to do what is needed of me.

And when you finally fly away
I'll be hoping that I served you well
For all the wisdom of a lifetime
No one can ever tell

In the days and years after Noah's death, I thought often about how we raised him. His disability figured large in his life and ours; it was an integral part of who we were as a family and how we planned and worked together. Caring for him was something that was a constant in our lives. Without us or another caregiver, Noah could not have gotten by in the world. As Noah flew away from us, I felt confident that we'd given him the kind of life that any kid would want to live. We loved him unconditionally, and we brought each other great joy every single day.

Grief and Moving Forward Stories

After great pain, a formal feeling comes—372
by Emily Dickinson

After great pain a formal feeling comes—
The nerves sit ceremonious like tombs;
The stiff Heart questions—was it He that bore?
And yesterday—or centuries before?
The feet, mechanical, go round
A wooden way
Of ground, or air, or ought,
Regardless grown,
A quartz contentment, like a stone.
This is the hour of lead
Remembered if outlived,
As freezing persons recollect the snow—
First chill, then stupor, then the letting go.

chapter 20 | A Thousand Thoughts

Celebrating Father's Day with Bob.

ight months after he died, I made it through my first day without crying. The next morning when I realized it, I felt like I'd abandoned Noah. And I cried.

I wore a heavy cape of sadness. It was like a second skin that I could not shed. It was in my hair, on my hands, around my knees, and on my face. It was especially weighty on my shoulders. My posture took a curve forward, my chin was low, and I couldn't stand tall without effort, as if the light of the sun was too much for my eyes. Grief was inside me too, in my bones and heart.

After the funeral when I finally needed to go to the grocery store for coffee and milk—the only things friends and neighbors didn't bring us—I looked at people and their kids and was shocked at how sad and angry they made me feel. Without focus, I tearfully meandered from avocados to pears thinking, "How is it that you have a child to love, kiss and see grow up and my child is dead?" Around every aisle, it seemed like there were parents and kids, talking, laughing and saying no to candy and cookies, like I once did with Noah. I turned away, so they wouldn't see me looking at them or crying.

Later, while pumping gas, I saw a grandfather and his grandson standing at the station near a big beige Buick. The man coached the bright and eager-faced boy on how to hold the nozzle and fill the tank. I cried there, right at the station. These tears were for my dad, who would never spend any more time with his grandson. I cried for me, too, because the kid wore a forest green winter jacket that looked like one of Noah's.

When he died, Noah came to live more fully in my consciousness. Instead of him being physically present every day at home, I pulled him into my mind with the purpose of keeping him alive. The anticipatory wince he made when we ducked him and his wheelchair into the van; the *ah* sound he made after a sneeze; the smell of his head; the sound of his quiet laugh as he told us a joke; the bright, peridot green color of his eyes. I knew that I would never experience those specific, lovely things ever again and that made me cry. Every time I thought about him either living or dead, I cried. I wondered if I might ever stop feeling so purely sad. Sometimes I cried hard and long and my stomach hurt from it. Other times I had what I can only call *crybursts*. I'd cry just for an instant—a minute or two—and then carry on with whatever I was doing as if nothing had happened at all. Sometimes when I was driving and had miles of undistracted time to think of him and our life together, I'd have to pull over to the side of the road. I couldn't see because I was crying so hard that my face and neck hurt from the tension.

I ran the day Noah died and the day after. I ran the morning of his funeral, too. Running gave me respite from the unexpected flood of cards, flowers, plants and dropped-off meals. I was grateful for all of those thoughtful things, but I was made sadder by the handwritten notes, the pervasive scent of roses and lilies and each bite of someone's homemade sympathy pie.

The solitude of running provided a space for me to think about Noah without distraction. After a mile, my legs pumped along effortlessly and my mind could finally wander. It was always a random thought of him, something not connected to anything at all—like the first time he sipped from a straw. I remembered so clearly his surprise at the new taste of a root beer float. As that image infiltrated my mind, I'd start to cry and the run became effortful. My breathing became a huff-huff-huff instead of huh-huh-huh and I ran and cried, wiping my nose on a glove or a sleeve as I traveled the grass along the channel and the boardwalk near the Lake Michigan beach. Before going to sleep, I would try to write in my journal. But that which was supposed to provide solace made me feel more desolate and lonely, so I only wrote a few sentences, if any.

I thought about him in thousand different ways after he died. I thought about him more often than I did when he was alive. I had seventeen years of memories to keep in my grip, and I didn't want to lose a single one of them.

chapter 21 | The Gifts

Bob, Roberta and Elaine King, circa 1963.

took only one of the Lorazepam pills my doctor prescribed to help me sleep. Those tiny pills were so potent, yet ineffective, that when I awoke and got up for a glass of water I staggered around the bedroom, unbalanced, stumbling, reaching out for a wall that evaded my hand. I didn't like that out-of-control feeling and threw the pills away. While the pills might have helped me sleep, they wouldn't deaden the permanent pain.

Thinking of Noah caused my jaw to tense, my throat to tighten. Without warning, tears would slip down my face like beads from a broken necklace. In the privacy of the shower with the fan running and door locked, I moaned and sobbed, doubled over in the hot water. Other times I bit the inside of my lip bloody or poked a plastic mechanical pencil under my fingernail. I hoped the physical pain would negate the agony in my heart.

I was on US 31, driving up north to have lunch with a friend and my MINI took off when I floored it, moving quickly from seventy miles per hour to ninety on the empty expressway. I passed a few cars and a semi and I edged it up to about ninety-two, thinking, *What the hell? I've got nothing to lose. My son is dead. If I die, I'll see him again.* I drove another mile or so at ninety-five, watching Michigan's grey-turning-to-green-post-winter landscape fly by. I slowed down. The cars I'd passed came into sight in my rearview mirror. I wasn't really reckless. Careless, sometimes. Reckless, never.

It seemed necessary to test the boundaries of normal living, now that nothing seemed normal without Noah. Even when I played with danger, deep down, I always knew that something kept me tied to this life, my family, my true and pragmatic self.

If the love and support of our parents and our upbringing shape our character, resilience, behavior and reactions, then I know why I didn't *go there* after Noah died. Nature—yes there was some of that. But nurture gave me what I needed to manage my emotions after his death. My parents were not prone to histrionics of any sort, maybe some dramatic storytelling by my mom, the schoolteacher, but no fits of rage, no broiling arguments or drama of any sort. Shaped by my dad's World War II service and their shared post-Depression upbringing, they believed that life's challenges were to be reviewed, managed and worked through. I grew up with those ideals as my guideposts. My parents expected me to be independent, resilient and self-sufficient, strong in character and will.

I am fully aware that resilience isn't the only option. A friend told me about her cousin, who also lost a child. The cousin took to her bed day after day, sleeping, crying, and shunning her family and friends. She finally rose for the child's funeral and had an emotional breakdown there in the presence of family and friends. I note this because I believe it is a legitimate and honest reaction. I worried and wondered if this might happen to me, that I would have an unexpected emotional explosion, triggered by Noah's death. I could almost, but not quite, envision it. I felt it coming in those days following his death. It was a loose, high-pitched feeling, a flutter in my chest that came and went. In the end, my emotions were too tucked in for a reaction of that magnitude.

❖

When vexed by my behavior, my mom and dad, like other parents of baby boomers, consulted *Dr. Spock's Baby and Child Care* book. As suggested by the book, my parents indulged me and raised me to believe I was smart, capable, and above all, special. I was the center of their universe, or believed I was. It was apparent that my mom and dad didn't need any other kids. I was enough. It wasn't until I was a teen that I thought to ask why I didn't have siblings. "There were supposed to be three or more kids after you—but you were such a child that I went on the pill the first year it was offered," my mother said. If nothing else, she was straightforward.

Without siblings and with parents who worked, I *had* to be independent and self-reliant. If my friends weren't around, I amused myself. I could read for hours, work on a craft project, play with my Barbie, chat with my cat or build a fort in the vacant lot behind our house without any companionship at all. The idyllic 1960s were seemingly safe, and my trusty Schwinn bike and I would set out on a summer morning in search of new places and friends. I discovered kids and playgrounds miles from my home only returning for food and candy money. It wasn't that my parents didn't care or wonder about my whereabouts, but I always found my way home and that seemed to satisfy their need for safety.

We spent a lot of time together, the three of us. We talked current events over meals, took car vacations across the East Coast and south to visit America's historic sites and went to Lutheran church on Sundays. My dad read to me every single night before I went to sleep. It was a very quiet and ordinary childhood.

I was seven years old when my parents dropped me off at Girl Scout camp. It wasn't my first time away from home, but it was my first with people who weren't family. After placing me, along with my brand new official Girl Scout mess kit and flannel-lined sleeping bag, into my four-girl tent, my parents headed down the wooded path for the car. I ran after them bursting into sobs. A hug from my dad was followed up by my mom's advice: "Get ahold of yourself. This is just two weeks of camp. Go make some friends, and earn some badges. Stop wailing, you'll be fine."

Crying and carrying on was acceptable, but it had its limits.

I wasn't born with the strength and ability to manage life's defeats and victories. I learned and practiced it growing up; it was instilled in me every day by my sensible, loving parents. When Noah died, I so badly wanted to melt down. I wanted to shriek, tear my clothing and take to my bed, quit my job, or go on a bender, but something inside, an internal rudder guided me in a different direction. Everything my parents gave me—those gifts of strength, resilience, compassion and love—surfaced and pulled me over the big waves that threatened to drown me during the desolate post-death days and I am thankful for that, for them.

chapter 22 | Leave of Absence

Noah's Holy Card.

After the visitation and funeral, a deep, quiet and frightful emptiness came over everything/life/me. When a parent, grandparent or spouse dies there are workplace rules that apply. You take care of *business* and it's back to *business* in a week, give or take, depending on your relationship to the deceased. But when a child dies, none of the ordinary rules apply. I suspect that the section in personnel policies about the number of leave days allowed for specific deaths don't even include children.

"Take as long as you need," my boss, Diana, told me. I stayed home for two weeks after the funeral, developing a somewhat comforting routine to fill the emptiness and sadness. After a restless night of sleep, I'd help get Tasha ready for school, paying her some of the attention that used to belong to Noah by making her breakfast or driving her to school. Suddenly, she was an only child and our sad parental attention—or more accurately— inattention was all hers. During Noah's time in the hospital, she was pretty much beyond our radar screen. She stayed with whatever willing family we could find. Her godparents, aunt and uncle, former daycare provider and friends all provided a place for her and made sure she got to school each day. And now it was just Mike, Tasha and me.

Noah's funeral was on Friday, and Mike went back to work on Monday. His work as a maintenance manager was a distraction for him, and his friend Karl was there to talk with him. "I don't know what I'd do if I stayed home," he said.

During my leave, as soon as it was light, I'd run five or six miles. I craved the Lake Michigan scenery near my house. I loved the solitude and hoped for the possibility of endorphins if I ran hard enough. Lost in my own thoughts, I'd focus on Noah and some shared moment of his life, but mostly I thought about his death and how god awfully I missed him. I'd cry while running and sometimes wondered when cars passed me and saw the agony and contortion on my face, if people didn't think that running was the most miserable sport a human could endure.

After an hour of running, I returned home, showered, made coffee and moved to the back of the house where I wrote thank you notes, standing up at Mike's worktable. It was the perfect height for writing and it was away from the kitchen and living room where flowers, cards and food were gathering. I'd spread out the cards, stamps and the guestbook from the funeral and visitation, and start writing notes with the heavy, comfortable and juicy (but not sloppy) pen that the funeral home gave me. It was green and gold with a rubbery pad to keep fingers from getting calloused or sore. I looked out the window, took in the little bit of southern sun that managed to squeeze through the winter clouds, and I wrote. Between notes I wandered the flower-filled, plant-filled house crying or trying not to cry. I'd return to the desk, look at my list of people who needed notes and I'd take the comfortable funeral home pen and write something kind. I thanked people who wrote notes on sympathy cards—like John who told me that he was sorry that I was living every parent's worst nightmare. *That* deserved a note. He was right. I was living a nightmare and I believed I'd be able to write my way into a more normal state of being. This old-school tradition of writing a thank you note made me feel strong. I tried to return comfort to people who offered me comfort. I wanted people who received the notes to think good things about Noah.

There were so many people to thank. Not just the people who sent flowers and plants for the funeral or gave memorial gifts, but also our neighbors who organized and brought complete meals and bottles of wine for two weeks—many of them cooking vegetarian meals for the first time. Joe and Jean from down the street brought a dinner and the most amazing six-inch tall lemon meringue pie, which was like a slice of sunshine in a Michigan March, so often grey, cold, damp and dirty.

I wrote to Dan and to his boss at the funeral home. I wrote to our parish priest and the new deacon assigned to our parish, whose first official church duty was to come to the hospital and help give Noah his last rites in the hospital and two weeks later to assist at his funeral. I wrote to the people who helped at Noah's funeral. I wrote to my cousin Todd from Livonia who, much to my astonishment, drove three hours and appeared at the funeral though I'd not seen him in at least fifteen years. I wrote to people who offered Masses in Noah's memory. I wrote to people who said very kind things at the funeral or left us small mementos. It felt good to write and connect with people without having to see them face-to-face. It felt good to be grateful, when there seemed little in life to be grateful for. I told myself that I'd go back to work when I was done writing.

I blew through a box of one hundred cards that were part of Noah's funeral package and the entire roll of stamps my dad had picked up for me. I drove over to the store and bought another box of twenty cards, stopping at the post office for a book of stamps.

The anxiety and tension from Noah's death, visitation and funeral made recalling details difficult, so the guestbook provided an abundance of information, like spouse and bus driver names that had slipped from my mind. Things I once knew easily, quickly, before Noah's death were just gone from my brain now. The book's addresses made the tedious envelope addressing much easier, too.

While looking for someone's address in the guest book I thumbed over an unfamiliar name, *Linda A.* and in in the address section, it said *Egg Roll House*. I smiled. She was a waitress at the Chinese restaurant where we went to eat with Noah. I don't think I ever knew her name. We'd been going there since Noah was a little kid. Linda must have spotted his photo in the obituary. She was at the visitation arriving right after friends from high school, Sheila and Jim. I called Mike to ask if he remembered talking to or seeing Linda. He didn't. I walked around the house a bit, letting this act of kindness settle in. It was so sweet, so tender of her to come to the visitation. I couldn't stop thinking about her. I could picture her face, too-dark for-her-age hair, her reading glasses on a chain and how she joked around with us when she brought Noah his egg rolls and glass of milk with a straw. Noah must have meant something to her and that mattered to me, so I wrote and told her so.

chapter 23 | Permanent Reminder

Noah's lock on the Artist's Bridge, Paris.

don't ever recall a specific conversation Mike and I might have had about having Noah's remains cremated. I'm sure at some point the conversation took place, but when Dan arrived at the hospital, Mike and I already knew what would take place. Neither of us liked the idea of Noah's remains going into the cold, dark February earth. Not that a fiery demise to his body was much better, but there are only two options. It was his precious body that we'd kissed, hugged, washed, carried, lifted, propped and adjusted for seventeen years, and what happened to the remains of his skinny self mattered. At least with his ashes, we could keep him close to us, rather than in a distant cemetery that we'd be less apt to visit. Even if we had put his remains in the nearby Lakeside Cemetery, I knew life would get in the way and we wouldn't visit as often as we intended.

Cemeteries are a permanent reminder that someone walked this earth and passed from it. Even after a few hundred years, headstones reveal faded names and someone like me can walk past, note a familiar name, a date important in one's own life or perhaps see an interesting cross, icon or carving. Even though I don't know the people buried there, I know they were here, walking the earth, just as I am.

I admire Italian and French cemeteries, where photographs of the dead are incorporated into headstones and objects are scattered about, refreshed every season by family members. Virgin Mary icons and saint statues are abundant, and entire extended families rest in peace in close proximity. When we visit Key West, we walk through the cemetery there with its iconic angel and above ground crypts on the island's coral bed.

My grandparents rest in Ogdensburg Cemetery near Traverse City, Michigan. Their plots overlook the water and vineyards of Grand Traverse Bay toward Bower's Harbor where they owned a little cottage when I was a child. But despite my fondness for cemeteries I just could not send Noah's body to one.

Noah's ashy remains are in a simple wooden box on an antique commode (not a chamber pot, but a fancy decorated chest with drawers) at the top of the spiral stairs in our house. It is in an airy room that serves as our home office and library. Much of the room's light comes from three north-facing windows and two stories of east facing glass brick.

Objects that decorate the space include Noah's fourth grade school picture—my personal favorite. In the photo he's beaming, looking heavenward and is wearing the school uniform of a white shirt and a knit navy vest. His little gold stud earring is visible, as is the back of his long, curly hair. Yes, he had kind of a mullet, before mullets were scorned. He's smiling and it is one of the finest school-issue portraits ever done. There's a small statue of the Virgin Mary and baby Jesus and a white porcelain bisque figure of an angel with spread wings encircling two children, several pink painted roses near the base of it. Tasha brought it home from school a few weeks after Noah died. Her class had taken a trip to the dollar store and she found it there. "That's me and Noah in there," she said as she placed it near the ash box. There is also a postcard of a Joan Miro painting and a couple of cast coins—one with a star, the other with a heart. Atop the box is a Mexican angel along with SpongeBob and Dash figurines.

After Noah died, I had an artist make a vase to go near the ashes. I had intended to put a few flowers there every day. In reality, though, it's closer to every couple of months, when I think to stop at the florist, and always in the spring when we have an abundance of daffodils and tulips in the yard. This is precisely why we couldn't bury Noah. I don't think we could have kept a visiting routine that would satisfy our need to be near him. At least with his ashes and small altar atop the stairs, I can make a brief visit every day.

Before we put the box on the home altar, Mike opened it and removed some ashes so we could share them in special places. He put them in a round tin box he'd had since he was a kid. We drove up to Bay Cliff in early June before camp began for the summer to place some of his ashes there. The drive was different than when we'd brought Noah with us—still melancholy—but more final. I wondered if we'd ever come back up to the camp again. A few staff people walked around with us, remembering places Noah liked to be and talking about things he said and did as a camper. Some of his ashes went into in a flower garden and some were sprinkled near the big gazebo in the center of camp. The gazebo was close to *Sam's Place* which was Noah's cabin there. We walked and talked about Noah and his years at camp.

We let some ashes fall into the ocean from a moat wall around Fort Jefferson in the Florida Keys. We'd visited the old fort with Noah a few times, pushing his wheelchair bumpily along that wall in the blistering sunshine. It was a place where we wanted to remember he had been with us. We dropped ashes in the Gulf of Mexico in Lignumvitae Key Channel, a place we'd boated with Noah just the spring before. We rented a boat and ventured into the warm, turquoise and sparkling waters where we thought Noah would like to be. A shadowy stingray passed under us shortly after we poured the ashes in the water. We put some in our friend Joy's garden in Oceana County, just north of us. Noah spent a lot of time with us at Joy's and she asked that some of him remain there with her.

While I'm not willing, at least at this point in time, to put Noah's ashes into a cemetery, I have found ways to create permanent reminders of him. I don't want him to be forgotten after Mike and I are dead. I want his name to live on, not only in people's memories, but some place where people might see his name and remember him in the same way gravestones from years ago evoke the person buried there. When the City of Muskegon began to place benches on the Muskegon Lake Channel wall, we funded one. On the back of the blue bench is a small cast aluminum plaque that is inscribed:

Noah W. Miesch
Blufftonite Big Red Parrothead
Missed every minute
Mom, Dad and Tasha

The bench is just in front of our house overlooking an inlet. As people read the inscription they can look across the water and see the house where Noah lived. We look out our kitchen window and see people reading the plaque, sitting on the bench, or using it to hold tackle boxes while they fish.

In the years following Noah's death, we found long distance travel to be an acceptable diversion from our grief. Seeing new cities, viewing lovely landscapes and amazing art, eating good food and meeting people helped dull the pain. For a few weeks, we could ignore the depth of our sadness and distract ourselves from the reminders of Noah that were scattered around our house and in our lives. We made it to Europe twice by the fourth anniversary of his death, once to visit Italy and bike from Rome to Florence and another trip to bike in Provence and visit Paris and Barcelona. The trip to France and Spain was planned to coincide with Noah's birthday on September 23 and a Jimmy Buffett show in Paris on September 24, 2010.

"If we could get tickets," I said to Mike, "it would be so much fun to go, don't you think?"

"We were just in Italy a year ago," Mike said. "But, it would be cool to see Buffett in Paris."

"I know. It'd be a once in a lifetime thing and we'd be away for Noah's birthday. I might not be able to get tickets anyway, it probably will sell out fast. But, I'm going to try. Noah would want us to go," I said.

He agreed, and when tickets went on sale, some seven months before the show, I easily bought two. "If the rest of trip doesn't pan out, or we find we can't afford it, I can always sell the tickets or just not use them," I said, hoping that wouldn't happen.

Our equally impulsive California friends, Veronica and Kirk, decided to meet us in Paris. While they're not Parrotheads, they're Deadheads and that seemed to be a good enough reason for them to join us for the Buffett show.

While trip planning, I spotted an article about people putting locks on the Pont de l'Archeveche Bridge over the Seine River.

According to the writer, people place small padlocks on the bridge as a symbol of eternal love. While Parisians don't love the idea of their bridge being all locked up, visitors do, and Mike found a lock that we packed into our suitcase.

On Noah's birthday, we attended Mass at Notre Dame Cathedral with Veronica and our former next-door neighbors, Thom and Janet, who also happened to be in Paris. After Mass and lunch, we made our way to the bridge. Thom and Janet knew Noah well and provided a lively narrative of memories as we locked the *Noah M.* engraved lock onto the bridge. I'm sure the lock is gone by now, cut off by a Paris municipal worker, as we heard they were apt to do. That afternoon though, in honor of Noah's twenty-second birthday, we created something permanent for our memories.

Noah liked wearing rings and was wearing a simple one when he died. We'd bought the ring up north, in Marquette, when we were bringing him home from camp. It was cheap and the metal turned his finger green because he wore it all the time. During the hours after Noah died and while we were still at the hospital Jodi, from Child Life, offered to make a plaster relief of his hand and foot for us. The fragile castings sit on the dresser in Noah's room.

Before Noah died, he and I had talked about getting a class ring. He liked wearing rings and already had a Muskegon Big Reds varsity jacket. A ring would complete his high school prepster persona. His hands were small, though and I wondered if we'd be able to get a man's ring to fit him. It might have been that ring permanently imprinted in plaster that reminded me of the class ring we were going to get, or perhaps it was the melancholy of back-to-school season in September, but in the end, a mailer from Josten's that likely went to all juniors at Noah's high school arrived in the mail. I looked over the various options, used the ring sizer on my left middle finger and found some designs I liked that would make a nice ring for us. I chose a classic men's ring in yellow gold with an academic crest and his name on one side and a dolphin and his graduation year, 2008, on the other. The dolphin was a reminder of his dolphin swim and our *Floridays* as we called them. The ring features a blue stone for his birth month of September and his name is inscribed on the inside. I wear it when I run races, for good luck, and sometimes kiss it for extra power. It is my permanent reminder. People ask about it sometimes. Young people will often ask if it is mine. I just tell them it belonged to my son, but I'm wearing it now.

When I die, I'd like to have my ashes and Mike's buried in a cemetery somewhere, with Noah's. We'll have a nice headstone inscribed with our three names, so even when this paper I've written on yellows and fades away and this story is forgotten, there will be something mostly permanent in this world that affirms we all walked this earth together.

chapter 24 | Favorite Things

Father and son.

After Noah died, Mike and I promised each other that we would talk about him every day. "It'll help us both remember the details of his life and will let him know we are thinking of him," I said. In the weeks following Noah's death, we developed a routine during our hour-long, pre-dawn run. It went like this: we'd talk about the weather and how cold and/or windy it was, then onto politics and what was illogical about the other side's thinking, then a conversation about our daughter and her issues, complaints about or praise for work/co-workers, and as we neared Beach Street, turning toward the north with its bracing wind, during the last mile we'd talk about Noah.

At first, we relived the hours and moments of his last days. A scene was stuck in my mind and I wanted, needed, to talk about it. It was when Noah began to die. We came into his hospital room and the medical staff was upping his oxygen and frantically searching for better-fitting breathing masks. "Enough, he's done. Let him go," Mike said. It was incredibly brave and I know I couldn't have said it. I felt that Mike needed to know that his compassionate action at that moment to enforce our Do Not Resuscitate orders was still the best decision for our son.

We talked about how Noah showed great courage at death, how despite almost dying several times prior, he took control of the last moments of life and died when he was ready. There were hundreds of minutes that day we relived, evaluated and analyzed.

Over time, our running conversations migrated toward the seventeen years we had with Noah, instead of his death.

"He was so skinny," I'd start.

"And he never outgrew any of his clothes width-wise. He got longer, but never wider," Mike said. "And those footie pajamas we got him when he was ten, we had to cut the feet off, but they still fit him around the waist."

"Yep, he was the only seventeen-year-old wearing polar bear pattern almost-footie pajamas."

We'd talk back and forth for a mile or so about random, usually funny and wonderful things about Noah.

One morning when we were out running and talking about Noah, a troubling thought came to me.

"I feel bad about something," I said.

"What?" He was expecting that it might something big, like we should have moved Noah from the medium-sized children's hospital to a bigger place like Chicago or Detroit for more aggressive treatment or that we were slow to understand how sick he really was. But it was simpler than that.

"Noah asked me a bunch of times to make him spaghetti with syrup." I said. "Like Buddy in the movie *Elf* would eat. I refused to do it. I should have cooked some up for him. It would have made him so happy." We stopped running. I bent over crying on the side of the dark road, and Mike stood close with his hand rubbing my back. I could hear him crying, too. Other days there were different stories that would end the run early or slow us to a walk.

Years have passed since his death, and we still talk about him every day. Noah comes up in conversations more randomly now. We've moved toward mentioning things Noah liked or didn't like, based on *our* lens of his life. I'll make Pad Thai and Mike will remind me, "Noah never really liked your Pad Thai." True, he did not like it. I tried to make him think it was a pasta dish. He knew it was something else.

Sometimes we'll even debate what Noah would have liked or not liked. Mike might say, "Noah would have liked this." And I'll think *not* and, if needed, present a counterpoint. I don't wonder why we do this. We've grown into it for comfort or to keep the promise of talking about him every day.

When we're making a decision about an action, for example, a paint color, new furniture, or a travel destination, one of us is likely to say, "Noah would like this," or "Noah would want us to go there." He's always a part of us that way. When we're looking for an excuse to eat cheese, have a cupcake, or enjoy another drink, we'll say, "Noah would want us to…" and we usually do.

When Noah was alive and if Mike and I were talking about someone that Noah didn't know, he would interject, "I don't know him." He had a funny way of saying the word *him* it sounded more like *heem*. When one of us is talking about someone, it isn't uncommon for the other to say, "I don't know him," accent on *heem* included, instead of "Who are you talking about?"

When a Jimmy Buffett song comes on the stereo one of us will say, "Noah liked that song." And we agree that "Jolly Mon Sing" was his favorite Buffett song. When we plan our trips out of the dark Michigan winter that coincide with the anniversary of his death, we'll talk about how much Noah loved the Florida Keys and the places he liked best. We know he would have loved our new wiener dog, Lucy, and we imagine how fun it would have been to put peanut butter on Noah's very ticklish feet and let her lick it off. We try to imagine Noah alive and in our life now, wondering what he might look or sound like if he'd not died at seventeen.

"Pencil thin moustache," Mike will suggest.

"A very nice girlfriend."

"We'd have to de-kid-ify his bedroom."

Usually our conversations end there because imagining him now is difficult. When something ends so clearly, so abruptly, it is just done. Imagining is fun for a bit, but then it seems pointless, like imagining what you might do with lottery winnings when you don't even buy tickets.

On September 23, seven months and three days after he died, on what would have been Noah's eighteenth birthday, we held a little celebration. Neither of us could let the day go by without doing something. We just weren't sure what to do. There are no rules or protocol about what to do on the birthday of a dead child. So we had some friends for dinner and bought a cake from Ryke's Bakery, where we always get our birthday cakes. Mike went to the bakery to order it. The cake was decorated in green and blue plaid, and in frosting it read *Love You Always, Noah*. "I wasn't sure what it was supposed to have written on it. This seemed most true," he said. We didn't sing "Happy Birthday" or light candles, but we all made birthday toasts with our drinks before we cut the cake, trying not to look at each other as we cried.

Not long ago, I put on a John Prine CD while we were driving. The song *"Long Monday"* came on. Within the first few lines of the song Mike said, "This song reminds me of Noah."

"Why?" I asked. I didn't think we had the CD before Noah died. "Because he died on a Monday. It was a long Monday."

After five years without Noah it is clear to me that Mike misses him more than I do. I know that comparing one parent's reaction to loss to another parent's isn't fair, but I see it. I see it in the overwhelming sadness he feels and the ever-present funk he's suffered since the day our son died. No pill will fix Mike's mood, and I doubt he would take that pill if there were one. I see it when he stares off to the right of the old blue recliner where we have photos of Noah on a lamp table. One of the photos shows the three of us at a wedding; another is of Noah in the backyard wearing a red mock turtleneck shirt with our old shed in the background. There is a school photo—Noah looking shy and biting his lower lip with his bangs showing freshly combed little tracks. Often, Mike picks up one of the photos and looks closely at it, slowly setting it down. I see his grief in how he rearranges things in Noah's room, which is virtually unchanged since the day he left for the hospital. A few objects have been moved and a few objects, which Mike bought because he thought Noah would have liked them, have been added to the already crowded bedroom. One day, a coconut that was carved to look like a pirate appeared on his dresser. I knew where it came from and why.

During the last few years of Noah's life, Mike cut back his hours at work so he could be home at 3 o'clock when the school bus arrived. Even in high school Noah had to have someone there to lower the lift and take his wheelchair off the bus. So every afternoon Mike and Noah had a life without me until I got home from work. They'd mess around in the yard or house, shoveling or raking, having a snack and watching television. They both thought SpongeBob was the funniest thing. I imagined them watching it together, saying the lines ahead of the characters and laughing at the puns, jokes and mishaps.

If I'd known we only had a short time with Noah I might have stayed home more, too. I could have asked for a more flexible work schedule and watched SpongeBob with him. But it never occurred to either of us that Noah would leave us so soon. Oddly, in all of his years seeing various medical specialists no one ever mentioned, implied or hinted to us he was destined for a short life. Even his pediatrician, whom we saw a couple of times a year, never said anything and we never thought to ask. Were we naïve? I'm not sure. Perhaps no doctor would have predicted the future for us. If they had, I doubt we would have changed a thing.

In the years that Mike was home with Noah after school, they became incredibly close. Their time alone strengthened the bond, and their fondness for one another was apparent.

At night, though, or early in the morning when Noah awoke, he called for me.

"Mom? Mom! Mom?" he'd call persistently until I woke up and went downstairs to see what was wrong.

"What, Noah?" I would say, sleepily standing at his bedside at 2 a.m.

Sometimes he'd complain of pain, "My hips hurt." I'd put a small pillow between his knees and prop him as best I could. If he were cold, I'd find an extra blanket and tuck it all around him. Sometimes I'd put socks on his chilly hands.

But most of the time when he called me to his bedside he'd just say, "I love you."

"That's it? Well, I love you, too, Noah. Now go back to sleep and don't call me anymore. Save the next *I love you* for morning."

"Okay," he'd reply making a kissing sound. I'd kiss his head and go back upstairs to my own bed and he would settle into sleep. He called me almost every night, sometimes twice a night for seven or eight years. Though it made me sleepy during the day, it was a sliver of time with him that I own, and I'm glad he called for me.

CHAPTER 25 | Let it Be

Madonna and Child by Pietro Perugino.

While looking for something else in the nightstand drawer, I found a bookmark Noah made for me in the fourth grade. It was twelve inches long—too long to be practical—created of pink construction paper with his school photo laminated onto it and a hole punched above the photo with curling ribbon through the hole like a tassel. On the back, someone had helped Noah print, in a thickish pencil, "Happy Mother's Day, Love Noah." I imagine every mom of a school-age kid has such an item. I never used it much, but finding it after his death was like a prize.

A month before my first Mother's Day without Noah, I began to fret. I told Mike I didn't want to do anything special—I didn't want a card, presents or brunch at a restaurant. Mother's Day would be treated like any other Sunday. I just wanted it to pass quickly. It was Noah that made me a mother, and without him, I wondered if I was still a mom.

Yes, there was Tasha. But the bond she and I had was different than the bond between Noah and me. I'd hoped and expected it to be more, for the bond to be stronger, but it simply wasn't. We worked hard to connect with her, but the reality was we were little more than caregivers. As a former foster child, and older adoptee, she was too old, too damaged to want motherly nurturing and love. The love we gave her just rebounded and rarely was reciprocated. The years of neglect Tasha suffered at the hands of her biological family made her want for only the most basic things: food, sleep and safety. Even as she grew older, her needs remained very basic. She never sought a mother's love from me, though it was, and will always be hers for the taking. Noah's death added to the emotional gap between us. I couldn't help her understand the philosophical *why* of his death when I could barely make sense of it myself.

Mike respected my wishes regarding the first Mother's Day non-celebration. The day before, though, he bought some bright spring tulips for the vase near Noah's ashes. He put them up there without a word. Mother's Day morning I was thinking hard about Noah and some of the best times being his mom—taking photographs of him, choosing books to read together, washing his hair, going boating and eating quiet meals at home. There were many good days, and I did my best to focus on those fine days instead of the new normal—sadness, grief and loss.

I hoped that going to Mass on Mother's Day might help provide me with some comfort. It was the Virgin Mary that brought Noah and me to the Catholic Church. I was raised a Lutheran, but have always been attracted to the Catholic faith, and I can trace it to my love of art. I find Renaissance paintings of the Holy Family in museums, cathedrals and churches mesmerizing. I love the expressions of the figures: Joseph often looking distracted and tired for the most part—a minor figure in the big event. He is the father of the Christ child, but not really *the* father. Mary is most often looking straight at the viewer and is always serene. She's strong and focused, while little Jesus is sometimes playing and rarely making direct eye contact.

When I was working at Grand Rapids Art Museum we mounted an exhibition by the Italian Renaissance painter, Perugino. My favorite painting of the Virgin Mary and Christ Child was his creation. Mary is dressed in a dusty red garment and a deep blue robe with dramatic folds and shading. In the shoulder of the robe is a golden sun symbol. She stares straight out from the painting. Her eyes look slightly sleepy and her eyelids show as much as the brown irises do. She looks content and relaxed, as if this destiny to be the mother of God was not such a big event. Her lips are like a bow—almost pursed—and her cheeks are pink, like her mouth. She has tiny coils of hair around her neck, and the hair appears to be blown by a breeze. On her lap, baby Jesus is naked and chubby. He's looking off, distracted. His right foot is bracing on Mary's leg, like babies often do when pushing off or testing their strength. The long fingers from Mary's hands are around his waist and another lightly touches his leg with a thumb on his knee.

If the power of art can change a culture or move us to a deeper understanding of the world, I'm not embarrassed that it was great art that brought me to explore Catholicism.

❖

Tasha opted not to join me at Mass on that first Mother's Day. She was in her *I hate Jesus* phase and I was relieved to leave her at home. As I sat in the church Noah-less and child-less that first Mother's Day, it felt to me like Hallmark had taken over the service, which was ripe with motherly platitudes. I wanted to cry and at times during the Mass, I bit my lip and tried not to burst into great sobs as I wiped tears and my nose on my sleeve. Perhaps Catholics have a greater emphasis on motherhood because of the Virgin Mary—the epitome of a mother.

I believe that Mary understands a mother's grief. She knows what it is like to lose a son, so I prayed to her almost exclusively for help and solace after Noah's death. The night we came home without Noah for good, I was deep in the cold of loss and despair. I didn't know how to think about what had just happened and how we would move forward from that point. I prayed to Mary for clarity and strength. I trusted she would help me. It wasn't that I didn't think Jesus himself would or could help, but there are times when another mother's help is needed most.

"Dear Mary," I prayed crossing myself as I shook from fatigue and emptiness under the down comforter in our bed. I asked her to look after Noah, to keep an eye out for him in heaven. I knew he was there. I was concerned that Noah might be scared or upset to find himself in a strange place. After all, I had promised him when he was dying that people would know him in heaven. I needed Mary, another mom, to come forward and greet him.

Sitting in that church on Mother's Day, I missed being Noah's mother. I missed his presence at Mass, where he would hold my hand and we'd share the hymnal. I missed taking him up to the altar for Eucharist and helping him cross himself when his elbows were too tight to do it alone. Noah and I were confirmed, together, only about three years before he died. When I decided to start attending Mass, Noah came along willingly and happily. He liked the people who shook his hand and said hello. Father Mike always took an extra minute to talk with Noah, and Noah looked forward to seeing him each Sunday. And when he was ill and I knew he was going to die, I was thankful we had a home church and a priest who knew us.

I felt my sorrow turn to anger that there was so little regard for women who weren't mothers, or women whose mothers had died or for mothers whose children who died. At the end of the service, all the mothers were invited to come to the altar and take a small geranium plant. I exited out the back and hoped to avoid shaking hands with Father Mike, but a gap in the parishioners exiting brought me face to face with him. He held my hand for a moment and softly said, "It'll be all right." I burst into tears and dashed for my car.

I fell in and out of sleep that night and continued to pray for their meeting, visualizing my Mary's face in paintings. I wanted to say the rosary, but I couldn't remember the words, so I remembered the words to The Beatles' *Let it Be* and called on Mary in times of trouble. The song ran through my head as I drifted into dreams. I was hopeful then, and still believe that Mary and Noah found each other in the vast expanse of heaven and that she is looking after my son.

chapter 26 | A Crush On Him

A knowing smile.

People knew Noah. A trip to the grocery store, the Farmer's Market or a walk along the Muskegon Lake-Lake Michigan channel often included a stop to talk with a stranger or two. "Hi, Noah!" an enthusiastic adult or kid would say. Small talk would follow and I'd eventually have to introduce myself.

"I'm Noah's mom. And how do you know Noah?"

"Oh, we're friends at school."

"We met at the Y."

"Noah was at Pioneer Trails Camp with me one summer."

"I was Noah's substitute bus driver last year."

People remembered Noah. Most of the time he remembered them, too. When he didn't, he'd confess: "I don't remember them."

"That's okay, lots of people remember you, and that's pretty cool isn't it?"

"I think so," he said.

One summer evening we went for dinner at City Café. It was a hip, modern place in the lower level of the Frauenthal Center in downtown Muskegon, quite upscale for our community. It was our go-to spot for celebratory meals—birthdays, anniversaries and holidays like Valentine's or Mother's Day.

The elevator in the Frauenthal traveled only one floor, so for fun, we'd put Noah in the lift, push the interior button to "B" and, when the doors closed, we'd race down the steps, greeting him when the door opened into the restaurant.

"Noah! What a surprise to see you here. Would you like to join us for supper?" one of us would say. He played along, acting surprised and accepting our invitation.

While we were looking over the menu, a sweet, melodic voice greeted Noah.

"Hello Noah! How are you? So good to see you." Noah's face lit up.

"Hi!" he said, as he wiggled in his wheelchair. Noah and the stranger—our waiter—talked for a minute until he introduced himself. He was slightly built with short, sandy brown hair, pale skin, bright blue eyes behind glasses and a broad forehead with expressive eyebrows.

"I'm Damien. When Noah was at Bluffton School, I was in high school and I volunteered in his kindergarten classroom. Noah and I go way back," he said patting Noah's shoulder.

"So, Noah? Tell me about your Bluffton friends. Do you still see Regina and Abby? How is Pretty Kitty? You need to tell her 'hi' for me," he said.

"I will. I promise," said Noah.

That night, our family fell in love with Damien. He is that rare kind of waiter who knows how to respond to happy and unhappy people and did so with confidence and charm. He is energetic and moves easily, even gracefully, and never needs to write down his orders. His frequent smile is genuine.

Everything Damien said and did left an impression on us. He served us our drinks and meal, and we enjoyed the extra attention he was giving Noah.

"Bye, Noah," he said, bending over to give him a hug when we were ready to leave. "Come back soon and see me."

"I will," Noah said.

We returned to the restaurant often. Sometimes Damien would be working, sometimes not. When he was, we'd ask to sit in his section, and he'd greet us with his memory of our last drink order, "Roberta, a glass of Syrah tonight? A Blue Moon for Mike, and I bet Noah would like chocolate milk." Noah beamed and wiggled with the special treatment. When we couldn't get into his section he'd spot us, stop by to say hello, give Noah a hug and then dash off to serve his other tables. He'd check in as he passed to make sure we were in good shape. He introduced Noah to his managers as "my good friend." Eventually anytime we'd come to the host stand at the restaurant, we didn't have to ask for Damien's section. Staff would see Noah and know where to seat us.

Around the time of Noah's sixteenth birthday, I asked him what he wanted to do to celebrate. "Let's go out to eat," he said.

"Where do you want to want to go for dinner on your birthday?" I asked, knowing the answer, but asking to be polite.

"City Café."

"Sounds great. Maybe if we're lucky Damien will be working."

"I have a crush on him," Noah said.

I paused. This was an odd thing to say. Or maybe not, the more I thought about it.

"I hear you Noah. He's truly the sweetest guy. Having a crush on him is a good thing," I said.

Noah smiled and blushed a little.

Over the years people have told me that Noah was a flirt. I've heard it from his peers, teachers, physicians, therapists, nurses and friends—people say that he was charming and subtle, throwing smiles and giving hugs to people of both genders and all ages.

When Noah told me he had a crush on Damien, I wasn't concerned in any way. People who exude love and kindness are magnetic—people are attracted to them. In Damien, Noah met his magnetic match.

After Noah's death, we got brave and went to City Café for dinner. Damien greeted us with tears and hugs.

"I read about Noah's death in the paper. I don't know what to do. I'm so sorry. I can't believe Noah is gone. I'll miss him," he said. We all were wiping our eyes, sniffling and trying to stay composed in his workplace and among his other customers. We told him how Noah had passed bravely into death and that we guided him as best we could. "It won't be the same here without him," he said. "I always looked forward to seeing him."

"Damien, a few years ago Noah said the funniest thing to me. Right before his birthday dinner here, he told me he had a crush on you," I said.

Damien's eyes filled again and he began to cry outright. He put his hand over his mouth. He walked away to the kitchen and, after what seemed like a long time, returned to his floor and to his tables.

City Café was sold a few years ago and its old owners brought Damien and other staff over to their restaurant across town. We go there for special occasions like Noah's birthday and always ask for Damien because we have a crush on him still.

chapter 27 | Snapshot

Noah at seventeen years old.

took the photo in mid-January. Noah had been sick with pneumonia throughout most of December—back and forth to the doctor for appointments, rechecks and a series of chest x-rays. He missed quite a few school days before and after the holidays. Christmas vacation was tough; he looked thin, stressed and pale during the two-week holiday. The lack of oxygen and coughing made him tired and crabby. The whole family was at odds due to missed work, sleepless nights and the worry from caring for a sick kid. Just after the New Year he rallied.

"I want to go back to school," he said one morning.

"We're going to the doctor today, and it will be up to him. I'm hoping you can go back, too," I said.

"I miss my friends. I'm bored."

"Let's see what happens. You sound good, not so much coughing last night. Cross your fingers."

"Crossed," he said.

He was cleared to return to school. The next morning he was awake early, ready to go. He wanted to wear his favorite fleece, a bright green Gap hoodie. It was my favorite, too. It looked good on him. As he was waiting for us to take him out to the bus, I decided to shoot a photograph. His eyes were bright and his skin had color—his face looked happy.

"Hold on Noah, I want to take a photo. You look so robust today."

He sat up a bit straighter in his wheelchair and practiced a smile. I took a few photos.

His bleached blonde hair showed from under the hood of his fleece. The hair color was his idea. We had taken him to see

Murderball, a documentary about a wheelchair rugby team; the guys in it were handsome, tough and funny. One rugby player had bleached blonde hair and he and Noah looked alike, slender and boyish; we all noticed the resemblance.

"I want hair like that," he said after the movie.

"Bleached blonde?"

"Or purple. I'd like purple hair," he said.

"No purple hair. I think I could live with a blonder blonde," I said.

Together we picked out a box of hair bleach at Walgreens, and before he got sick, we bleached it. A towhead from birth, the new color was brighter than his normal shade of blonde. It was an odd, yellowish blonde. He liked it. I got used to it.

Noah smiled for the photo. It was not his normal big goofy photograph-for-mom smile, but a smaller, more tentative smile.

"Nice," I said. I showed him the thumbnail photo on the back of the camera.

"Good one, Mom."

And he was off to school.

❖

The framed photo sits on my desk at work and we have a 5x7 on the refrigerator at home. It was shot close-up, the mole under his right eye is visible as is a sprinkling of freckles across his nose. His eyebrows are dark compared to his bright hair and his green eyes look directly into the camera. His smile shows his teeth, quite nice and straight. The hoodie partly covers one side of his face more than the other and he shows a slight double chin.

He died seven weeks later. Despite looking healthy—he was harboring a lung infection he could not fight.

The photograph evokes memory. I look at it and visualize that precise moment when I took the camera and carefully set up the shot, thinking that everything was going to be okay.

chapter 28 | Dirty Clothes

Noah's varsity jacket and academic number.

n the bottom drawer of a dresser in our bedroom, I keep two Ziploc bags with some of Noah's dirty clothes inside—a t-shirt, a pair of mittens, some hand splints and a winter hat. They smell just like Noah. I wish there were more items, but I washed things too soon after he died.

When I'm longing, I'll open the bags and breathe in the scent that is him.

We have a DVD of him at summer camp and once a year or so Mike and I will play it. We can hear his voice and see him zipping around in his wheelchair with his friends; he looks so happy, tan and independent. We have at least a thousand photographs of him; I started taking pictures of him the day he was born until just a few weeks before he died. We keep our favorite images of him throughout the house and in our offices.

What I really miss, though, is his smell. I think because we had to lift him so much, and to lift safely is to hold close, I was always very conscious of his scent. I could tell by how he smelled if he'd been sweating at night, if he'd eaten garlic or if he'd gone swimming at the Y. I could tell if we'd used a scented soap in the shower or if the clothes he was wearing had just come off the clothesline or out of a plastic box for the change of season. I loved the smell of his head. Through the mess of blonde curls I could detect a little bit of sweat, a little oil, and the flowery smell of Aveda shampoo mixed with the scent of clean air from the pillowcase. His hands were always clenched because of cerebral palsy and they smelled damp, but never dirty—more like something he'd held and then eaten—like an apple slice. At times they would smell like a crayon or pencil he had used in school. Often his hands smelled like neoprene from his hand splints. When I would kiss him good night after reading I'd lean over and take in some of the air around him. It was sweet and soft, almost undetectable to anyone other than a mother.

After all these years the dirty clothes in the sealed bags still smell potent. When I'm missing him more than usual, I'll go to the dresser drawer, opening one bag I'll breathe in the air, then seal it up quickly. I don't want the scent of Noah to be diluted by new air. They don't contain notes of grass, licorice, chocolate, fall leaves or beach air like wine does. The bags smell like love, that's all. Just love.

chapter 29 | Virgin Feet

Barely worn.

L ike most of the other things that belonged to Noah, his shoes are still in the same place we left them when he died. They're stashed on a wire shelf in his bedroom closet with books, board games, kites, toy cars, stuffed animals and other things we don't have the heart to throw or give away. It seems like parents of kids who die are of one of two minds—there are *box it up and change up the bedroom* parents and *don't touch the room* parents. Over time, we gave away a few things—videos, a race car set and other odd toys. My goddaughter Charlie receives some of his books each year along with new books for her library. Most of the older books are inscribed, "To Noah with love, Mom and Dad." I find a clean spot in each book and inscribe it to her. I hope when she grows up she'll look at the doubly inscribed books and ask, "Who is Noah?" and I'll be able to tell her about him.

There's a shelf in his room that's a shoe shrine. Brown leather Arizona Birkenstocks for summer, lime green water shoes for wearing in the Florida Keys, and green and blue Chuck Taylors for school are all lined up together. He asked for a pair of fringed buckskin souvenir shop moccasins when were on a trip to the Upper Peninsula and wore those for the summer and into fall. His last year of high school, he chose a pair of Van's slip on sneakers with a skull and crossbones mashed up with the face of Che Guevara. They were tough looking teen shoes. They're all there, shoes like new, almost pristine.

Even as a seventeen-year-old boy, Noah's feet were soft like a baby's. A toe occasionally would get a blister or a callous from an orthotic that had not been padded correctly, or from the rub of a new shoe, but for the most part they were unblemished and perfect.

His feet were ticklish, and when we pulled off his socks and barely touched his soft and smooth arches, his foot would fly up.

"Don't. Stop it," he'd say breathlessly.

Parents love to find that special spot on their child that makes them wiggle, shriek and run away—but then, return for more of that crazy, loud affection. But a child who can't escape is even more fun to tickle; they're at your mercy and only can try to roll and snake away. Such it was with Noah. He'd thrash like a fish, pleading for me to quit it and when he'd stop laughing, he'd ask for more.

"Do it again."

The soles of his long and narrow feet were a tactile joy; they were not only tender and soft, they were sometimes damp and slightly stinky. They were sinewy from the tone brought on by his cerebral palsy, and if I rubbed them, they would relax a bit. Sometimes I'd use some peppermint foot lotion to make his soft feet even softer. His feet tended to be cold. When he was very young he pronounced the word cubes as *dubes*. To tease, I'd tell him his feet felt like dubes. He'd correct me, "Cubes, Mom. Ice cubes." He slept with socks on for extra warmth—the foot rubbing got the blood flowing to his feet and warmed them up, but not quite enough. Using a reflexology chart from a health food store, I'd press and hold his big toe or the ball of his foot, hoping to make his weak lungs stronger.

His dad called them virgin feet because Noah never walked—his disability saw to that. Throughout his life Noah stood only for a few minutes in any shoes. He took a hundred or so steps with the help of various physical therapy contraptions, but he never wandered around our house. He never walked through the snow or ran down our dirt road to catch the school bus. He never splashed on the shore of the beach near our house. That wasn't meant to be. His wheelchair parts needed replacing more often than his shoes did.

Each year we changed, fixed or repaired worn tires and broken brakes and bought him new shoes, just for fun.

chapter 30 | Christmas Eve Ass Reaming

Christmas lights.

The Christmas after Noah's death we didn't go to many parties; baking cookies didn't happen and I stopped sending out cards. For years I'd sent Christmas cards with Noah's photos in them. I made cards by hand sometimes, gluing a photo onto a card with a watercolor painted frame or onto a piece of color penciled cardboard. Noah was so angelic, so cute, that I couldn't resist showing him off to people who didn't see him every day. Now, I couldn't imagine signing a card that didn't include his name, so I didn't.

After Christmas Eve dinner, a brief and stilted family event, we decided to leave for Mass early and drive around Muskegon and look at the Christmas lights. There was a foot of new snow on the ground, and it was a cold and oddly windless night. We planned to drive through Bluffton-Beachwood and look at the luminarias and check out some of the more spectacular home light displays on Ireland Street, Torrent Avenue and Lakeshore Drive. Lastly, we'd drive down Jefferson Street where the window of each big Victorian house held a single electric candle. It was a Christmas lights tour we'd driven every year since Noah was a toddler.

In my red MINI Cooper with Tasha in the back seat and Mike as the passenger, we drove out along the shore of Lake Michigan from our house, taking a left down Waterworks Street past Noah's old school, Bluffton Elementary. The luminarias were brightly shining and there were hundreds of them. "So pretty," I said. "This is just the nicest thing." I was hoping that the comfort of our tradition would lift our collective Christmas spirits. But, of course, life doesn't work that way.

As we rounded the corner near the Muskegon Yacht Club on Cherry and Edgewater, a movement caught my attention. There were two teenage boys stomping on the luminarias. I hit the brakes on the car, skidded a bit on the packed snow, and leapt from the car. The boys began to run.

"Hey! Get back here. Stop. Come here, right now," I shouted. There I stood, a strange woman, ankle deep in the snow demanding two boys to stop and listen to what they surely must have known was trouble. Oddly, they did. The boy closest to me stopped. The other one who was further away looked like he was about to run. "Get over here," I demanded. He edged cautiously closer to his friend and the two of them came to me. I felt like I possessed a superhuman power that made delinquent boys listen to me.

"What the hell do you think you are doing? What gives you the right to stomp on these things?"

"I dunno," said the kid closest to me.

"What do you mean *you dunno*? You were stomping on these luminarias. You know what you were doing. You were destroying these lights. Look at this mess," I pointed to a half dozen crushed luminarias. "Does this make you feel good or something?"

"No," said one of the boys.

"Then why the hell did you do it?" Deep down, I knew this was a crazy question. Of all the human beings who act without understanding their motivations, adolescent boys are probably the most notorious. But I was on a roll, so I ignored common sense and the possibility that I heard giggling coming from the car and I let it play out.

"I dunno. It was his idea," the closer boy pointed to his friend.

"So he has a stupid idea and you just go along with it? And you're throwing your friend under the bus. That's nice. Was this really your idea?" I said, turning to the other boy.

"No," said the boy who had tried to run.

"What's your name? Where do you live? Where do you go to school?"

The boys told me their names. They were both freshmen at Muskegon High School. The boy closest to me, the one I'd seen doing the stomping acted as the spokesperson. "I'm in the freshman honors program at Muskegon," he said. As if this would give him favor with me.

"Really? That seems improbable. Are they just letting anyone into that program? People like you are honors students?" I said, giving him my best smarmy voice.

"No, I have a 3.75 GPA. Really, I do."

"I doubt that. If you're so smart then why are you out on Christmas Eve stomping on decorations? Who's the principal for the honors program?"

"Mrs. Blake-Edwards."

"Ah, I know her well. Maybe I should call her when school starts and let her know how you spent Christmas Eve, running around Bluffton stomping on decorations." This seemed on par with the threat of the Permanent Record, that apocryphal school menace that kept fearful teenagers in line, just as Santa's Naughty List had worked on Noah.

"No, please don't call her," he said.

"Maybe I should call the police or your mothers." I should have let them go, but it seemed that a little fear right now might stop these boys from a life of crime.

"Mike, give me my cell phone!" I said in the direction of the MINI. Mike had rolled down the windows to hear what was going on and he handed out the phone without a word. I imagined what he might be thinking in there and what he might be telling Tasha.

"Dad, make her get in the car," Tasha would ask. "I'm so embarrassed. She's so mean."

"Me? I can't make her to do anything," he would say.

"Please don't call the police," the boy said.

"I feel like I should. This pisses me off. People who live around here, people who care, took time doing all this decorating for Christmas, made all these lights and you just come along and stomp them out."

Why these boys didn't run, I'll never know. But they stood right there, in the snow and cold at 9:30 on Christmas Eve and took a seven-minute verbal beating.

"Mike, give me some paper and a pen." From the car window came a pen and a map.

"Give me your phone numbers."

They complied, and with shaky hands I wrote their numbers down. I didn't know what I was thinking or doing. Words had been flying out of my mouth, unfiltered, and my brain wasn't involved one bit. I must have had some authoritative look to these boys, and I felt the power of righteous indignation, but I was really just reacting to the moment.

"Give me your address," I demanded of the stomper.

"I don't remember it."

"What?! How can you not know your address? You're in the honors program. You just told me you were an honor student and you don't even know your own address."

"My mom just moved here."

"Where's your dad?"

"They're divorced."

"Ah hah! That makes sense. Figures you're from a broken home. They're divorced and you're out destroying things."

This was probably the meanest, most unfair thing I could say—blaming this kid's behavior on his parent's divorce and rubbing his face in it. I realized I'd said too much and, feeling regretful and ashamed, I toned it down a touch.

"So, what do you think your mom would say about this?" I said quietly.

"She'd be really mad at me. Please don't call her. She'll kill me," he replied.

"I can't blame her, think about her for a minute. New house, new neighborhood, divorce and you, her honor student is out on Christmas Eve stomping lights. Maybe I should just take you both home."

"We can't get them in the car," said Mike who was finally contributing to the scene. He was right. The MINI could only seat four people and as I pondered Mike's reply, I weighed the severity of two crimes: luminaria smashing vs. kidnapping. I knew I had to let them go.

"I can walk home. I promise we won't smash any more lights."

"What about you?" I said to the friend.

"I'm done smashing. I'm freezing. I need to get home, too."

"Are you going to call my mom?" said the kid.

"I'm on my way to church. I'll think about it for a while, maybe I'll pray about it. You, take yourselves home," I said.

"Thanks," he said. "I'm really sorry I did it," the boy said.

"When I come back after church, I'm driving by here and if there are any more lights smashed I will call your mother. I mean it."

The boys hurried off, across some backyards making tracks in the new snow.

"They're idiots," I said to Mike.

"What asses," he replied.

"I never saw a thing," he said. "All of a sudden you were jumping out of the car and yelling and then those kids just appeared. If I'd been them I would have hauled ass away from you, not toward you. I swear I never saw them do a thing," he said.

"This kind of crap makes me so mad," I said. I was almost crying.

"Dumb kids," Mike said.

My heart was still racing and my hands shook as I drove off down Lakeshore Drive passing more luminaria carefully set out and undisturbed. We drove the route as planned, admiring the decorated houses and the light displays, but I couldn't take my mind off those kids and the stomped luminaria—or the image of myself as the Christmas Eve Righter of Wrongs.

Mass was crowded, but we were still early enough to take the pew where I normally sat with Noah. I prayed to not be so angry. It wasn't right to be so mad, to be internally boiling and furious about what a couple of kids had done. They hadn't done real and permanent harm to anything other than to smash a few paper sacks and some candles. Eventually I calmed down, and the familiarity of the carols and the ritual of the Christmas Eve mass took my mind off the boys.

It has become common knowledge that anger is one of the stages of grief. My misplaced anger toward those boys was just anger about losing Noah. I couldn't very well lash out at Noah for dying or at the healthcare providers for not curing him. Mike and I had made the decision to let him go when he was ready and when he left us, it was of his own doing. So that Christmas Eve when those two not-very-innocent boys took a verbal beating from a mother in deep grief—which of course they didn't know— it wasn't about the luminarias at all.

I imagine us meeting again. If I'm lucky, they might thank me for setting them on the path of good and civil behavior, and I would thank them too, for letting me act out my anger at the loss of my son.

chapter 31 | He Plays a Harp

Mother's locket.

"Do you have any kids?" It is a perfectly innocent question. It comes up when I meet new people and goes with equally harmless questions including, "What do you do?" or "Where do you work?" or "Where do you live?"

I always say yes to the kid question because I have two children. Follow-up questions are where things get dicey. "How old?" or "Boys or girls?" I say that Noah is seventeen years old. He died at seventeen and he stands still there. As each year goes by without him, I grow older and he remains young. Things were complicated for a year when his sister Tasha was also seventeen, but she moved on. I imagine being seventy years old and the amazement and wonder of people when they ask me about my kids and I tell them I have a seventeen-year-old son. Perhaps when I get older, strangers won't ask about my kids anymore.

People who are well meaning or simply unaware tell me about their seventeen-year-old sons and daughters too—where they're planning to go to college, what high school sports they play and their extra curricular activities. They inquire about Noah's interests, too.

This presents a dilemma. I have to make a fast, instinctive decision about whether to drop the "my child died" bomb or to play along in a mysterious and evasive manner. My mental checklist plays out like this:

1. Will I ever see this person again? If not, there is no need to tell them anything. If I think I will, I need to be truthful.

2. Do I think they can handle the "my child died" bomb? There are some people I intuitively know will understand and others whose reactions I fear.

3. Do I feel like talking about Noah? I usually do.

Sometimes, though, my indecision or procrastination about what to say puts me on a collision course with truth. I was at a conference less than a year after Noah died, and over cocktails, a woman from an Eastern state asked about my kids. She was wiry with big glasses, which gave her a curious Mr. Magoo-like appearance. She was new to our group and she seemed to know everything about anything.

"My son is seventeen," I said.

"So is my son! I'll bet he's using your car and driving all the time now. My son is constantly gone," she said. I nodded. Noah's cerebral palsy prevented him from learning to drive (and walk, for that matter) so I couldn't relate. I agreed, though, that driving was a source of motherly angst. She asked about Noah's other interests and activities. "What is he taking in school?" "Does he play any sports?" "What extra curricular activities is he into?" "Does he have a girlfriend?"

I just didn't like her. I didn't want to tell her the truth about Noah. I just didn't need the emotional interaction that comes when I say, "My son is dead." Saying this *always* evokes an emotional reaction. Instead of telling her he was dead, I told her what I envisioned for his life had it not ended before our parental dreams could be realized. I took a sip of my martini and then took a deep breath.

"He'll be going to the University of Michigan when he graduates." My husband Mike and I loved Ann Arbor and had always imagined that Noah would go to school there. I faltered at his potential vocation—he'd always liked animals and space. I pondered whether to say veterinarian or astronaut as I wasn't sure if Michigan offered majors in either.

"He plays a harp," I said. *Where did this come from?* I thought as I said it. *A harp?* "He's a good Catholic, and he's very close to God," I said. My mouth and my imagination were working overtime.

"Is he considering the priesthood?" she asked.

"Yes, the priesthood is an option."

She stopped and didn't ask about his girlfriend.

I took something from that encounter. Most of the time when people start asking about my kids, I deflect their inquiries and move right to their kids, posing more questions than a police interrogator. When I've done a good job, I've asked enough questions so that people are either exhausted or so charmed by my interest that they don't ask a thing. Truthfully, I enjoy hearing about other people's kids. I understand the struggles parents face and the interesting choices young people at Noah's age are making at this critical juncture between childhood and adulthood.

While I often try to avoid the topic, I've also learned that not being honest about having a child who died leads to unexpected complications. The worst instance happened right after Noah's funeral. I went for a pedicure while on bereavement leave. I purposefully made a weekday appointment, expecting there would be fewer people at the salon than on a Saturday. I wasn't interested or able to make small talk with a stranger in the next pedicure chair when so much had happened to me just a few weeks before. I sat in the chair and leafed through a *People* magazine looking at celebrities with youthful, carefree faces and problems that were really not problems at all. Erin, the nail tech, did a fine job on my feet. She said very little, just some friendly small talk, and I responded politely. The problem came when I continue to see her every six weeks, and now we're so far down the road that I don't even know how to broach the subject of Noah. "Oh and by the way, my son died five years ago and I always meant to tell you." She knows a lot about my life, the work I do, my marriage, our travels, my running and my political views. She knows about the struggles with our daughter, and I know about her challenges with her two adopted kids, too. I consider her a friend. Yet this one big thing, the most significant event in my life, is a topic that I've never found the right moment to talk with her about it. When I put my feet in that bowl of soapy hot water for the first time, I never thought it would lead to this complicated sin of omission.

Imagine if there were a word for parents of kids who have died. People who lose a spouse are widows or widowers. When someone asks, they say, "I'm a widow." Everything is instantly clear. We know this person has lost a spouse and they are possibly still grieving. There is no doubt about what has happened. Orphans, too, have their own word. There are people who when asked about their parents, might reply, "I am an orphan." Or "I grew up as an orphan." Even the term "motherless daughter" is commonly used to describe girls or young women who lose their mothers to death before adulthood. These special words clearly tell the specific life circumstances of a person.

Parents with children who have died don't have a word of their own. I've tried to see if there is anything in etymology that might be adequate. The Latin word *Viduus*, which is where the word widow comes from, has 'bereft' and 'void' as its origins. Bereft is part of it, but being deprived of someone loved or valued just barely begins to touch the death of a child. In Sanskrit the word *viloma* could be used to describe us. It means "out of the natural order of things," which child death certainly is. I've tried to create a new word, thinking perhaps I could start a movement of parents who also feel the need, but I can't even land on a good definition, much less a word. I want one word that expresses the overwhelming sadness, absent dreams and unfinished stories that parents experience when a child we created, brought into the world and love deeply, still, is gone from our lives forever.

Acknowledgments

Roberta and Noah.

wish my mother, Elaine King, were still alive so she could know how her belief in me helped bring *He Plays a Harp* to publication. She never doubted that I could do whatever I wanted to, and though writing a book about the death of her grandson was likely not on her list, I know she is proud.

Thank you to Kristen Tennant who gave me the first little push to write Noah's story and to Adam Schuitema and Paula Nangle who over a few years read pieces, parts and finally the whole manuscript. Their ideas and input shaped the book from start to finish. I appreciate my first draft readers who told me how it was working, where it wasn't and pointed out my writing shortcomings—Amanda St. Pierre, Joan Huyser-Honig, Jane Clingman Scott, Beth Probst, Laura Yelsik and Caroline Leavitt. Special thanks to my English teacher at Western Michigan Christian High School, David Schelhaas, for encouraging me to write and helping me believe I had some talent. To my instructors at the UCLA Extension Writer's program, Gordon Grice, Liza Monroy, Dan Jaffe and especially Victoria Zackheim. Each of these people helped make me a better writer with their critiques and guidance. It was Jim McKean at the Iowa Summer Writing Festival who told me readers would want to know Noah through my stories. To Laurie Cirivello and Holly Becheri, who made a place for my writing in *The Rapidian* and published "Fearless," which made me believe I could write a book. To my editor, Lisa McNeilley, who prodded me to explain myself more fully and was masterful in her edits and to Dirk Wierenga for shepherding my manuscript along the publication path. Thanks to my enthusiastic running best friend and fellow author Lisa Rose Starner, and to my best friend in the community foundation world, Veronica Blake Lovejoy for always reminding me what Noah would want us to do. I'm grateful to my boss, Diana Sieger, who signed my reimbursement forms for writing conferences and writing class tuition and noticed my improved writing at work! And thanks to a great group of enthusiastic friends who never waivered in their support and always asked, "How's it coming?" They include Melissa Freye, Susan Maskell Alexander, Laura Caprara, Will Juntunen and Heidi Stukkie.

Parts of *He Plays a Harp* appeared in these publications and are gratefully acknowledged: *Atticus Review, Brain, Child: The Magazine for Thinking Mothers, The Boiler Review, Hippocampus, Lifelines* (The literary journal of The Geisel School of Medicine at Dartmouth College) and in *The Rapidian*.

About the Author

Roberta F. King works as the Vice President of PR & Marketing at Grand Rapids Community Foundation. Outside of her professional public relations writing her articles and essays have been published in: *Atticus Review, Brain, Child: The Magazine for Thinking Mothers, The Boiler Review, Hippocampus, Lifelines* (the literary journal of The Geisel School of Medicine at Dartmouth College) and in *The Rapidia*n.

Roberta graduated from Valparaiso University and has a Masters degree in Communication from Grand Valley State University. When she's not writing, she runs and enjoys road racing and inn-to-inn bicycle travel. She is proud to have been named Oceana County's Mrs. Asparagus Runner Up in 1989. She is presently completing a certificate in nonfiction through the writing program at UCLA Extension. *He Plays a Harp* is her first book. She and her husband Mike Miesch live on a small peninsula surrounded by Muskegon Lake and Lake Michigan in Muskegon, Michigan.

www.robertafking.com for news and events
Facebook: RobertaFKing
Twitter: @robertafking
Contact: he.plays.a.harp@gmail.com

About the Cover Art

The cover art is an oil pastel drawing by Mike Miesch, Noah's father. Mike has a BFA in printmaking from Grand Valley State University and attended the Slade School of Fine Art at University College London. His artwork appears infrequently at art shows in Western Michigan.